SCOTTISH PIETY
A MISCELLANY FROM FIVE CENTURIES

SCOTTISH PIETY

A Miscellany
from Five Centuries

A. C. Cheyne

Professor of Ecclesiastical History
and Principal of New College, Edinburgh

DUNEDIN ACADEMIC PRESS
Edinburgh

Published with the generous support of
The Drummond Trust, 3 Pitt Terrace, Stirling
and
The Hope Trust, 52 Moray Place, Edinburgh

Published by
Dunedin Academic Press Ltd
Hudson House
8 Albany Street
Edinburgh EH1 3QB
Scotland

ISBN 978-1-903765-78-4

British Library Cataloguing in Publication Data
A catalogue record for this book is available from the British Library

Typeset by Makar Publishing Production, Edinburgh
Printed and bound in Great Britain by Cromwell Press

Again,
with love and gratitude,
for Mona

'So near, inaccessible,
Absent and present so much.'

CONTENTS

TWENTIETH CENTURY

Preface

It is a surprising fact that, despite the multiplicity of scholarly works on Scottish church history which have appeared in recent decades, very little has been said about what religious men and women would have considered their deepest concerns. A host of erudite and perceptive writers have concentrated attention upon matters of law and politics, the social background, Church–State relations, Acts of Parliament and General Assemblies, doctrinal controversies and changes in public worship, but what one might call (in Wordsworth's phrase) 'the pulse of the machine' is scarcely touched upon, and the heart-beat of personal devotion goes almost unheard. There would seem to be room for something different – and the trail-blazing Professor Donaldson, most eminent of Scotland's historians, pointed the way forward when he suggested, in *The Faith of the Scots* that: 'The search must be made, not for men's actions, which are narrated in chronicles, but for their thoughts, which are related, if narrated at all, in private writings; not what is recorded in records, or survived in tangible structures and artefacts, but what lurked invisibly in human minds.' Following Donaldson's lead, the aim of the present anthology is to rescue from possible oblivion the views of the world which motivated and sustained Scottish Christians in past days – mot so much by examining their public and official utterances (though these could be the outward expression of deep-seated inner conviction, and may not be ignored) as by directing attention to their more private assumptions, attitudes and practices, and the life-style which grew out of them. Their prayers and praises within the home, their intimate communications with fellow-believers, their unstudied accounts of formative experiences, their considered tributes to memorable personalities, and their disclosures (not infrequently off-guard) of how they viewed the Power behind the universe: in these may perhaps be found the key to what is otherwise incomprehensible in the national history and – conceivably, a pointer to certain essentials of Christian living in any age.

A. C. Cheyne

Introduction

The many who knew and admired the Revd Professor Alec Cheyne – teacher, historian, pastor and preacher – will be grateful for this work, which he prepared in his final months. They will feel his gentle presence once again, and hear his voice, and be instructed, amused and inspired. Those who did not know the man will come to know him through this book, as he guides them through selections from some five centuries of Scottish devotional writing and helps them understand the rich religious tradition that shaped his life, and the lives of countless other Scots. Professor Cheyne was a highly respected historian of the Church, who devoted long years of reading, reflection and writing to the religious history of post-Reformation Scotland, and especially the Presbyterian Churches. He was a minister of the Church of Scotland, and a profound and eloquent preacher, who embodied the Scottish Presbyterian ideal of the learned clergymen, deeply rooted in Scripture and the traditions of the Church. And he was a man of culture, with a love of literature, music, travel and conversation – a man of broad interests, good humour and abiding sympathies. This book is his loving tribute to Scotland, and the religious influences that helped to form it. First, let me say a little about the book, and then a little more about the man.

❀ ❀ ❀

For centuries, the people of Scotland were shaped by the Christian faith. Their parish churches were centres of communal life, where people worshipped together, looked for divine guidance on how to order their lives, lifted their minds and hearts above the physical struggle for existence, learned to see eternal potential in each individual life, and contemplated the ultimate purpose and meaning behind all things. In the churches, the ancient rites of passage – baptisms, marriages and funerals – defined the stages of individual lives. In the churchyards, the ancestors were buried; their gravestones and funereal monuments symbolised the enduring bonds between the generations. Christianity provided hope in times of adversity, solace in times of bereavement, and inner strength amidst the trials of life, both great and small. It brought the joy and light of the ancient festivals. It gave the Scottish people, in their remote northern country, a sense of being part of a larger world civilisation. In hearing again and again the stories from the Christian Scriptures, generations of Scots felt an intimate connection with the peoples of ancient Palestine, Egypt and Assyria. There were, to be sure, darker aspects of Scotland's Christian faith. Some Scots saw only a God of wrath, quick to anger and capricious in his dealings with humankind. Some found in Christianity a reason to judge and condemn their neighbours, to persecute heretics, burn women for witchcraft, and wage holy wars. For many, their time in this world was only a stony path of pilgrimage, and their Christian faith demanded narrow, joyless and puritanical lives. These attitudes, too, had their role in shaping Scotland and its national character.

In truth, we know relatively little about the Christian faith of the vast majority of the Scottish people. Historians have described in considerable detail the religious conflicts and controversies of Scotland's past – the struggles surrounding the Reformation, the wars of the Covenants, the conflicts between Church and State, the theological debates and heresy trials, the clashes between different denominations of Christians. We know a great deal about the lives of John Knox, Thomas Chalmers, David Livingstone and other prominent Scottish Christians. Social historians of religion have discovered much about the changing patterns over time in church attendance, church membership and participation in church rites, and about the role of gender and social class in religious practice. But it is far more difficult to discern what people believed, what they thought about the universe and its ultimate purpose, how they approached death, and how the teachings of the Christian faith touched their innermost being. In this work of his old age – in these his final reflections as a historian – Professor Cheyne considered the beliefs of the Scottish people. The work is evocative, suggestive and impressionistic, rather than analytical, in its approach.

The book brings together a wide variety of devotional writings from Scotland's past – poems, paraphrases of psalms, liturgical guides, memoirs, anecdotal accounts, hymns and autobiographical writings. For each of the texts, Professor Cheyne provides a brief commentary, drawing upon his extensive knowledge of Scottish history and upon the experiences of his long career in Church and University. The selections progress chronologically from the sixteenth century through to the twentieth century. They were carefully chosen to illustrate important themes in Scottish piety – salvation through grace alone, martyrdom, the sacraments, preaching, the corporate recital of psalms, faith in the goodness of God, assurance amidst adversity, self-surrender, the imperative of mission, views of Scripture, family devotion, doubt, death and prayer. They were also meant to show how Scottish piety changed over time. Major figures from Scotland's religious history make their appearance – John Knox, Samuel Rutherford, Ebenezer Erskine, Thomas Chalmers, Robert Rainy, Henry Drummond, David Livingtone, Mary Slessor, John Baillie and George MacLeod. But there are also lesser known men and women – simple parish ministers, country schoolmasters, writers of paraphrases, makers of hymns and minor poets.

The devotional writings are drawn largely from a specific tradition – the Calvinist (or Reformed) and Presbyterian tradition of Scotland. There are, to be sure, some exceptions – Sir Walter Scott and J. G. Lockhart (Episcopalians) and Edwin Muir (a convert to Roman Catholicism) make their appearance, as does David Livingstone (a Congregationalist) and Thomas Carlyle (an honest doubter). But most of the passages reflect the Calvinist and Presbyterian tradition which for most of the past five centuries was predominant in Scotland. This tradition has been the subject of much criticism in recent decades – condemned for imposing a repressive puritanical morality and rigid Sabbatarianism, for stifling creativity in the arts, or for promoting intolerance towards other faiths. Some of this criticism was deserved. But as these writings illustrate, there was also much to admire in the Scottish Presbyterian tradition.

In an unpublished lecture on 'Calvinism in Scotland', probably prepared in the 1970s and found among his papers after his death, Professor Cheyne reflected on the nature of this tradition. He was by no means an uncritical observer, and he certainly did not accept all aspects of the Calvinist theological system as it was expressed in the Westminster Confession of Faith. But he did recognise its considerable strengths. This Calvinist tradition, he observed, gave the highest respect to Scripture as the expression of God's will for humankind and as providing all that is needed for human flourishing. It included the belief that men and women of all social orders could learn to read the Bible with understanding and know God's will for their lives. The scriptural emphasis, expressed in Bible readings, the sermon and the singing of the Psalms, formed the core of public worship in the Church of Scotland from the Reformation onwards. 'The essence of worship', Professor Cheyne observed, 'was to hear the Word, and respond to it in ways which the Word itself prescribed.'

The Calvinist tradition, he continued, was also infused with an 'overpowering sense of the majesty and omnipotence of God' – the God who had created the universe in all its vastness and complexity, who determined the laws of nature and society, and who directed all things for the higher good. This conception of the transcendent God could fill people with fear and trembling, especially in approaching the sacrament of the Lord's Supper. 'But', he added, 'in days of trial and testing, it also brought both confidence and endurance.' It could strengthen believers with the certainty that God ruled over all creation and that nothing happened by chance or accident. It could teach them to fear God and none other, and to put their trust in the Lord. The Calvinist tradition emphasised God's redemption of humankind through Christ's sacrifice on the cross. Human nature was weak and prone to sin. But God promised his help to the faithful, and through his divine grace the weak find strength, the despairing gain hope, and the sinful are steeled against temptation. This gave strength and support to countless individuals through the centuries.

As a system of church government, Scottish Presbyterianism is characterised by two salient points – the parity of all ministers, and government by a hierarchy of church courts. In the Presbyterian system, no minister exercises rule over another. The Presbyterian tradition includes the notion of Church and State as two sovereign societies (with both under the authority of God). Presbyterians do not accept that the State should ever exercise control over the Church. Rather, it is the responsibility of the Church to maintain its independent witness, and when required to admonish governments and politicians – fearlessly and without desire for favour – in the name of a higher morality. For most of the five centuries covered in this book, the Presbyterian tradition placed great emphasis on individual discipline. Christians were called to strict standards of moral behaviour, and discipline was enforced through the church courts. This discipline, to be sure, could be overly puritanical, and overshadow much that brought sweetness and light to the world. But the 'Calvinist ethic' could also focus energies, instil steady habits of work, and promote a commitment to excellence. Combined with the concern for discipline, Presbyterians fervently promoted education. They venerated learning in their ministers; they encouraged regular Bible study among their congregations; and they established schools, colleges and universities to enable individuals to achieve their potential and contribute to the best of their abilities to the commonwealth.

This Calvinist and Presbyterian tradition was only one among a number of religious traditions that helped to form the Scottish nation, and in emphasising this tradition, Professor Cheyne did not intend to downplay the vital contributions of the other great Christian traditions – the Roman Catholic, Episcopalian, Congregational, Baptist, Methodist, Quaker and many others. Nor should Professor Cheyne's volume be viewed as dismissive of the contributions of those Scots who could not accept the Christian faith. He emphasised the Calvinist and Presbyterian tradition because this was the tradition of the large majority of the Scottish people during these five centuries, and because this was the tradition that he knew most intimately.

The Calvinist and Presbyterian tradition has been waning in Scotland for several decades, and most dramatically since the 1960s. While it continues to shape numerous individual lives, it no longer wields the social influence and authority that it once did. Many of its churches have closed, and have been demolished or been diverted to other uses. Fewer young people are being nurtured within the tradition; many congregations are made up largely of older worshippers. But for most of the long period from the mid sixteenth to the mid twentieth centuries it was a powerful, living, defining force – a force that did much to enable Scotland to make contributions to world civilisation that were far disproportionate to the size of its population, and more important, a force that gave meaning to the lives of countless Scottish men and women, and encouraged them to see beyond the material universe and aspire after eternal truths.

❦ ❦ ❦

And now some brief discussion of the man. Alexander Campbell Cheyne was one of the best loved teachers and preachers of his generation, a man of eloquence, humanity, humility and gentle humour. One of his former students, Dr Richard A. Riesen, has recently published a memoir, and much of what follows is based on this work.[*] Alec Cheyne was born on 1 June 1924 in Errol, Perthshire. His father was a minister of the United Free Church (a Reformed and Presbyterian denomination that would unite with the Church of Scotland in 1929); his mother, who was from Inverness, was a cultivated woman from a distinguished family in Church and university. Before training

* R. A. Riesen, *Professor A. C. Cheyne: An Appreciation* (Edinburgh: Scottish Church History Society, 2006).

for the ministry, Alec's father had served as an officer in the Gordon Highlanders; he fought at the Somme, was badly wounded in the final German offensive in 1918, and was haunted for the rest of his life by the War. In 1928, his father became minister of a church in Kirkcaldy, in Fife, and it was here that Alec spent his boyhood. It was a cultured home. His father was an accomplished violinist, and encouraged his children in a love of music; his mother had a great love of literature and the house rang with literary discussion and debate.

Alec began his studies at the University of Edinburgh in 1942, in the dark days of the Second World War. He initially intended to study literature, but – inspired by the eloquent lectures of an eminent professor of history – he soon moved to history. He graduated MA with First Class Honours in history in 1946. This was followed by military service, then postgraduate study in history at the University of Oxford, and then an academic appointment in the Department of History at the University of Glasgow. After a few years of lecturing in history, however, he felt a calling to the ministry, and entered the Faculty of Divinity (New College) of the University of Edinburgh, earning his BD with Distinction in ecclesiastical history in 1956. He completed his probationary training for the ministry, and had every intention of becoming a parish minister in the Church of Scotland – but his scholarly abilities had made a great impression, and he was called back to New College to serve as lecturer in ecclesiastical history. He became Professor of Ecclesiastical History at the University of Edinburgh in 1964, a post he held until his retirement in 1986. He combined his work as a university professor with his vocation as a minister of the Church of Scotland, taking an active role in the Presbytery of Edinburgh (including service as Moderator of the Presbytery), and preaching regularly around Scotland and abroad.

Professor Cheyne was renowned as a lecturer. He lectured broadly on all aspects of the history of the Church, but it was his lectures in Scottish church history that were most memorable. His lectures were highly polished performances, beautifully structured and richly illustrated with anecdotes and quotations drawn from a wide variety of sources in theology and literature. He was able to draw his audiences into a past world, and breathe life into its personalities and debates. His lectures were infused with empathy for the human condition, and with much colour, description, humour and passion. The rhythms of his prose reflected his love both of poetry and of music. For many years, he taught (with a colleague in English Literature) a highly popular course on Scottish religion and literature. In 1983, he published a major study of religion and culture in nineteenth-century Scotland, *The Transforming of the Kirk: Victorian Scotland's Religious Revolution*. His long-standing fascination with Thomas Chalmers led in 1985 to a volume of essays, *The Practical and the Pious: Essays on Thomas Chalmers (1780–1847)*, which he gathered and edited. His introduction to that volume provided the best short study of Chalmers to be found anywhere. This was followed by his wide-ranging *Studies in Scottish Church History* in 1999. He also published a number of important scholarly articles in journals and edited volumes. He was honoured by his fellow historians, from Scotland and beyond, with a Festschrift in 2000 (*Scottish Christianity in the Modern World: In Honour of A. C. Cheyne*), and he was Honorary President of the Scottish Church History Society. As a historian, he was perhaps at his best with the essay format, which enabled him to convey the essentials of a historical theme or historical personality within a tight framework, and to make best use of his skill in writing precise and elegant English prose. He was rooted in the tradition of liberal historiography, with its emphasis on the importance of individual human actors, on the human potential for good, and on the value of human freedom.

My teacher and friend, Professor Alec Cheyne, died peacefully on 31 March 2006 in Peebles, amid the rolling southern hills that he had come to love. He compiled this collection in his final months, and he was very concerned that the voices of these faithful Scots – and these seekers after faith – be heard again, as in a choir of witnesses.

Stewart J. Brown
Professor of Ecclesiastical History
University of Edinburgh

Sixteenth
Century

ON THE RESURRECTION OF CHRIST

Done is a battell on the dragon blak,
Our campion Christ confountet hes his force.
The yettis of hell are brokin with a crak,
The sign triumphal rasit is of the croce,
The divillis trymmilis with hidous voce,
The saulis ar borrowit and to the blis can go,
Chryst with his blud our ransonis dois indoce:
Surrexit Dominus de sepulchro.

Dungin is the deadly dragon Lucifer,
The crewall serpent with the mortall stang;
The auld kene tegir with his teeth on char,
Quilk in a wait hes lyne for us so long,
Thinking to grip us in his clows strang;
The mercifull Lord wald nocht that it were so,
He made him for to felye of that fang;
Surrexit Dominus de sepulchro.

He for our saik that sufferit to be slain,
And lyk a lamb in sacrifice was dicht,
Is lyk a lyone rissin up agane,
And as gyane raxit him on hicht;
Sprungin is Aurora radius and bricht,
On loft is gone the glorious Appollo,
The blissfull day depairtit fro the nicht:
Surrexit Dominus de sepulchro.

The grit victour agane is rissin on hicht,
That for our querrell to the deth was woundit;
The sone that wox all paill now schynis bricht,
The dirknes clerit, our fayth is now refoundit;
The knell of mercy fra the hevin is soundit,
The Cristin ar deliverit of thair wo,
The Jowis and thair errour ar confoundit:
Surrexit dominus de sepulchro.

The fo is chasit, the battell is done ceis,
The presone brokin, the jewelleries fleit and flemit;
The weir is gon, confermit is the peis,
The fetteris lowsit and the dungeoun temit,
The ransoun maid, the presoneris redemit;
The field is win, ourcumin is the fo,
Dispulit of the tresur hat he yemit:
Surrexit Dominus de sepulchro.

W. Mackay Mackenzie (ed.),
The Poems of William Dunbar (1932, 1990), pp. 159–60.

yettis = gates; trymmillis = tremble; borrowit = redeemed;
indoce = endorse; dungin = beaten; stang = sting; kene = bold;
on char = open; felye = fail; was dicht = made ready;
gyane = giant; raxit him on hicht = raised him on high;
wox = waxed; jevellours fleit and flemit = jailors fled and
banished; weir is gon = war is over; lowsit = loosed;
dispulit = despoiled; yemit = kept

William Dunbar (?1456–?1513) was probably his country's greatest poet before Burns; but he remains a shadowy figure. The dates of his birth and his death are uncertain, the details of his education equally so, though he possibly studied at St Andrews. He may have been, for a time, a Franciscan friar; but as time passed he became more and more involved in court life. His first notable poem, 'The Thrissil and the Rose', celebrated the marriage of James IV and Margaret Tudor, which he had helped to negotiate. He enjoyed a royal pension, and seems to have taken part in various diplomatic missions to the Continent. As a writer, he could be either lyrical or (like many of his fellow-countrymen down the ages) devastatingly satirical. Capable at times of coarse vulgarity and fierce personal abuse, he could on other occasions give expression to the most ardent and moving piety.

Dunbar's masterly poem 'On the Resurrection of Christ', with its sonorous, bell-like repetition of the Latin words, 'Surrexit Dominus de Sepulchro', proclaims what has been the foundation and central message of Christian devotion in Scotland from the earliest times to the present day. It forms an eminently appropriate preface to this entire volume.

❦ ❦ ❦

A SPIRITUAL LOVE-SONG

All my hart, ay this is my sang
With doubill mirth and joy amang;
Sa blyith as byrd my God to sang:
Christ hes my hart ay.

Wha hes my hart bot hevennis King;
Quhilk causis me for joy to sing,
Quhome that I lufe atouir all thing:
Christ hes my hart ay.

He is fair, sober, and bening,
Sweit, meik, and gentill in all thing,
Maist worthiest to have loving:
Christ hes my hart ay.

For us that blissit bairne was borne;
For us he was baith rent and torne;
For us he was crownit with thorne;
Christ hes my hart ay.

For us he sched his precious blude;
For us he was naillit on the rude;
For us he in mony battell stude;
Christ hes my hart ay.

Nixt him, to lufe his Mother fair,
With steadfast hart, for evermair;
Scho bure the byrth, fred us from cair;
Christ hes my hart ay.

We pray to God that sittis abufe,
Fra him let never our hartis remufe,
Nor for na suddand worldly lufe:
Christ hes my hart ay.

He is the lufe of luifaris all,
He cummis on him quhen we call;
For us he drank the bitter gall:
Christ hes my hart ay.

I. Ross (ed.), *The Gude and Godlie Ballatis*
(1940/1957), pp. 40–1.

ay = always; atouir = above; bure = bore; lufe of luifaris = lovers

Although the first known edition of the *Gude and Godlie Ballatis* dates from 1567, earlier versions probably circulated in Scotland in the 1540s, when Lutheran influences were increasingly powerful. Authorship of the poems is generally attributed to three brothers from Dundee, John (principally), James and Robert Wedderburn. John, a contemporary of Patrick Hamilton at the University of St Andrews, may have served for a time as a priest in Dundee. After fleeing, at the end of the 1540s, to Luther's Wittenberg (where he was joined by his brothers), he later returned to Scotland, and may have survived into the post-Reformation era.

The book itself is a unique compound of doctrinal prose and poetry, 'Spiritual Sangis', 'Certain Ballatis of the Scripture', and – finally – 'The Psalmes of David, with other new Pleasand Ballatis'. Some of the contents are devotional, others satirical, yet others religious adaptations of popular songs; and their vogue in the pre-Reformation period seems to have been considerable, doing much to create a climate of thought which was both critical of the established Church and conducive to religious change. The Lutheran flavour of the whole is incontrovertible; yet much in the book has features common to both late-medieval Catholic piety and even the dominant Calvinism of the 1560s and subsequently.

In 1543 the Privy Council prohibited the 'making, writing, or printing of any such literature' and one can understand why; but the warmly evangelical tone of 'A Spiritual Love-Song' casts light on the new religion's world-changing potential, and its ability to 'cast the kingdoms old into another mould'.

❧ ❧ ❧
FAITH (NOT 'WORKS') THE ESSENTIAL

None of our works neither save us nor condemn us

It is proven that no works make us either righteous or unrighteous, good nor evil; but first we are good before that we do good works, and evil before that we do evil works: Ergo, no works neither save us nor condemn us. Thou wilt say then, Maketh it no matter what we do? I answer thee, Yes, for if thou doest evil, it is a sure argument that thou art evil, and wantest faith. If thou do good, it is an argument that thou art good and hast faith; for a good tree beareth good fruit, and an evil tree evil fruit. Yet good fruit maketh not the tree good, nor evil fruit the tree evil. So that man is good before he do good works, and evil before he do evil works.

The man is the tree: the works are the fruit. Faith maketh the good tree: Incredulity the evil tree. Such a tree, such a fruit: such man, such works. For all that is done in faith pleaseth God, and are good works; and all that is done without faith displeaseth God, and are evil works. Whosoever thinketh to be saved by his works, denieth Christ is our Saviour, that Christ died for him, and, finally, all things that belongeth unto Christ. For how is He thy Saviour, if thou mightest save thyself by thy works? Or to what end should He have died for thee, if any works of thine might have saved thee? What is this to say, Christ died for thee? It is that thou shouldest have died perpetually, and that Christ, to deliver thee from death, died for thee, and changed thy perpetual death in his death. For thou made the fault, and He suffered the pain, and that for the love He had for thee, before ever thou wert born, when thou hadst done neither good nor evil. Now, since He hath paid thy debt, thou diest not; no, thou canst not, but shouldst have been damned, if his death were not. But since He was punished for thee, thou shalt not be punished. Finally, He hath delivered thee from thy condemnation, and desireth nought of thee, but that thou shouldst acknowledge what he hath done for thee, and bear it in mind, and that thou wouldst help others for his sake, both in word and deed, even as He hath helped thee for naught, and without reward. O how ready would we be to help others, if we knew his gentleness and goodness towards us! He is a good and gentle Lord, and He doeth all things for nought. Let us, I beseech you, follow his footsteps, whom all the world ought to praise and worship. Amen.

'Patrick's Places', in W. C. Dickinson (ed.), *John Knox's History of the Reformation in Scotland*, vol. II (1949), p. 228.

Patrick Hamilton, a member of Scotland's lesser aristocracy, first encountered Lutheran opinions while studying at the universities of Paris and Louvain in the early 1520s. Returning home, he was incorporated as a post-graduate student at St Andrews, but did not clash with the ecclesiastical authorities until 1527, when Archbishop James Beaton accused him of being 'one who disputed and propounded . . . without proper commission . . . his own false doctrines, as well as the opinions of Martin Luther'. He left the country for Philip of Hesse's new university of Marburg; and it was there, under the influence of the Lutheran Francis Lambert, that he came to settled – and 'heretical' convictions. These he summarised in semi-academic language, shot through with ardent evangelical zeal, in what came to be popularly known as 'Patrick's Places'. At the heart of his argument (as shown in the extract given here) is an emphasis, not on the 'works' or acts of piety, which were central to much late-medieval devotion, but on the condition of people's hearts and their trust in Christ the Redeemer.

Hamilton returned to Scotland, and soon emerged as an enthusiastically proselytising reformer. Charged with heresy before the Archbishop's Council, he was condemned and burnt as a heretic in February 1528. Knox's *History of the Reformation* contains a detailed account of the trial and execution, including Hamilton's fateful words: 'I will not deny my beliefs for fear of your flames. I am content that my body should be burnt here rather than that my soul should burn in hell for denying my true faith. I appeal against the sentence of you bishops and doctors and take me to the mercy of God.' Hamilton's constancy, as Knox maintains, made a profound impression on those who saw or heard of it, so that 'almost within the whole realm there was none found who began not to enquire, Wherefore was Master Patrick Hamilton burned? . . . And so within short space many began to call in doubt that which before they held for a certain verity.'

❀ ❀ ❀
AN EXEMPLARY CHRISTIAN

(Emery Tylney's tribute to George Wishart)

About the year of our Lord one thousand five hundred and forty three, there was in the University of Cambridge one Maister George Wishart, commonly called Maister George of Bennet's [Corpus Christi] College, who was a man of tall stature, polled-headed, and on the same a round French cap of the best. Judged of melancholy complexion by his physiognomy, black-haired, long-bearded, comely of personage, well-spoken after his country of Scotland, courteous, lowly, lovely, glad to teach, desirous to learn, and was well-travelled; having on him for his habit of clothing, never but a mantle frieze gown to the shoes, a black Milan fustian doublet, and plain black hosen, coarse new canvas for his shirts, over white falling bands and cuffs at the hands, all the which apparel he gave to the poor; some weekly, some monthly, some quarterly, as he liked, saving his French cap, which he kept the whole year of my being with him. He was a man modest, temperate, fearing God, hating covetousness, for his charity had never end, night, noon nor day; he forbore one meal in three, one day in four for the most part, except something to comfort nature; he lay hard upon a puff of straw, coarse new canvas sheets, which when he changed he gave away. He loved me tenderly, and I him for my age as effectually. He taught with great modesty and gravity, so that some of his people thought him severe, and would have slain him, but the Lord was his defence. And he, after due correction for their malice, by good exhortation amended them, and he went his way. O that the Lord had left him to me, his poor boy, that he might have finished that he had begun! For in his religion he was, as you see here in the rest of his life, when he went into Scotland with divers of the nobility that came for a treaty to King Henry VIII. His learning was no less sufficient than his desire: always prest and ready to do good, in that he was able, both in the house privately and in the schools publicly, professing and reading divers authors. If I should declare his love to me and all men, his charity to the poor in giving, relieving, caring, helping, providing, yea infinitely studying how to do good unto all men and hurt to none, I should sooner want words than just cause to commend him. All this I testify with my whole heart and truth of this godly man.

John Foxe, *Acts and Monuments* (1563/1570), vol. V, p. 626.

Our picture of George Wishart (1513?–46) is largely dependent on accounts in Foxe's *Book of Martyrs* (which contains Tylney's tribute – from an admiring pupil) and Knox's *History of the Reformation*, and allowance must be made for the obvious bias of both in his favour. Wishart had a side to him which was very different from that which they present: like most sixteenth-century Reformers, he could indulge in the most virulent denunciations of those with whom he disagreed, and evidence is not lacking that he was the associate of men who would stick at nothing in their opposition to the Catholic clergy of the time. There is nevertheless a charm in Tylney's portrait of him which carries conviction, reminding us of the infectious, day-to-day piety which characterised Wishart's life, and helping to account for the affection of his friends as well as the courage with which he faced his horrifying death.

A MARTYR'S LAST WORDS

When that he [George Wishart] came to the fire, he sat down upon his knees, and rose again; and thrice he said these words, 'O Thou Saviour of the world, have mercy upon me: Father of Heaven, I commend my spirit into thy holy hands.' When he had made this prayer, he turned him to the people, and said these words: 'I beseech you, Christian brethren and sisters, that ye be not offended at the word of God for the affliction and torments which ye see already prepared for me. But I exhort you, that ye love the word of God, your salvation, and suffer patiently, and with a comfortable heart, for the word's sake, which is your undoubted salvation and everlasting comfort. Moreover, I pray you, show my brethren and sisters, which have heard me oft before, that they cease not nor leave off to learn the word of God, which I taught unto them, after the grace given unto me, for no troubles nor persecutions in this world, which lasteth not. And show unto them that my doctrine was no wives' fables, after the constitutions made by men; and if I had taught men's doctrine, I had got greater thanks by men. But for the word's sake, and true Evangel, which was given to me by the grace of God, I suffer this day by men, not sorrowfully, but with a glad heart and mind. For this cause I was sent, that I should suffer this fire for Christ's sake. Consider and behold my visage, ye shall not see me change my colour. This grim fire I fear not; and so I pray you for to do, if that any persecution come unto you for the word's sake; and not to fear them that slay the body, and afterward have no power to slay the soul. Some have said of me, that I taught that the soul of man should sleep until the last day; but I know surely, and my faith is such, that my soul shall sup with my Saviour this night, or it be six hours, for whom I suffer this.' Then he prayed for them which accused him, saying, 'I beseech the Father of Heaven to forgive them that have of any ignorance, or else of any evil mind, forged lies upon me; I forgive them with all my heart: I beseech Christ to forgive them that have condemned me to death this day ignorantly.' And last of all, he said to the people on this manner, 'I beseech you, brethren and sisters, to exhort your Prelates to the learning of the word of God, that they at the last may be ashamed to do evil, and learn to do good; and if they will not convert themselves from their wicked error, there shall hastily come upon them the wrath of God, which they shall not eschew.'

Many faithful words said he in the meantime, taking no heed or care of the cruel torments which were then prepared for him. Then, last of all, the hangman, that was his tormentor, sat down upon his knees and said, 'Sir, I pray you forgive me, for I am not guilty of your death.' To whom he answered, 'Come hither to me.' When he was come to him he kissed his cheek and said, 'Lo! Here is a token that I forgive thee. My heart, do thine office.' And then, by and by, he was put upon the gibbet, and hanged, and there burnt to powder. When that the people beheld the great tormenting of that innocent, they might not withhold from piteous mourning and complaining of that innocent lamb's slaughter.

W. C. Dickinson (ed.), *John Knox's History of the Reformation in Scotland*, vol. II (1949), pp. 244–5.

The very fact that this account of George Wishart's meek and conciliatory behaviour in his last hours comes from the pen of John Knox (no exemplar of the spirit of forgiveness) makes it all the more impressive and convincing.

Like many of his associates, Wishart seems to have been something of a cosmopolite, at home not only in his native Angus, the neighbouring town of Dundee and the Scottish Lowlands from Ayrshire to East Lothian, but also in the England of Archbishop Cranmer (though his time there was marred by a short-lived lapse into heresy), the Germany of Philip Melanchthon, and the Switzerland of Heinrich Bullinger.

His fame rests not only on his memorable and valiant preaching – sometimes, as in later Covenanting days, in the open air when the parish churches were closed to him – but on his translation of the first Helvetic Confession (1536), which introduced Scotland to a version of Reforming thought that paved the way for the reception of Calvinist insights in the succeeding generation.

A PROTESTANT MANIFESTO

(Preface to the Scots Confession, 1560)

The Confession of Faith professed and believed by the Protestants within the Realm of Scotland, published by them in Parliament, and by the Estates thereof ratified and approved as wholesome and sound doctrine, grounded upon the infallible truth of God's Word.

> **Matthew 24** *And these glad tidings of the Kingdom shall be preached through the whole world, for a Witness unto all Nations, and then shall the end come.*

The Preface

The Estates of Scotland, with the inhabitants of the same, professing Christ Jesus his Holy Evangel, to their natural countrymen, and to all other Realms and Nations, professing the same Lord Jesus with them, wish grace, peace, and mercy from God the Father of our Lord Jesus Christ, with the spirit of righteous judgment, for Salutation. Long have we thirsted, dear Brethren, to have notified unto the world the sum of that doctrine which we profess, and for the which we have sustained infamy and danger. But such has been the rage of Sathan against us, and against Christ Jesus his eternal verity, lately born amongst us, that to this day no time has been granted unto us to clear our consciences, as most gladly we would have done; for how we have been tossed a whole year past, the most part of Europe (as we suppose) does understand. But seeing that of the infinite goodness of our God (who never suffers his afflicted to be utterly confounded) above expectation we have obtained some rest and liberty, we could not but set forth this brief and plain Confession of such doctrine as is proponed unto us, and as we believe and profess, partly for satisfaction of our Brethren, whose hearts we doubt not have been and yet are wounded by the despiteful railing of such as yet have not learned to speak well; and partly for the stopping of the mouths of impudent blasphemers, who boldly condemn that which they have neither heard nor yet understand. Not that we judge that the cankered malice of such is able to be cured by this simple Confession: No, we know that the sweet savour of the Gospel is, and shall be, death to the sons of perdition. But we have chief respect to our weak and infirm brethren, to whom we would communicate the bottom of our hearts, lest that they be troubled or carried away by the diversities of rumours, which Sathan sparsis [spreads abroad] contrary to us, to the defecting of this our most godly enterprise; Protesting, that if any man will note in this our Confession any article or sentence repugning to God's holy word, that it would please him of his gentleness, and for Christian charity's sake, to admonish us of the same in writ; and We of our honour and fidelity do promise unto him satisfaction from the mouth of God (that is, from his holy Scriptures),or else reformation of that which he shall prove to be amiss. For God we take to record in our consciences, that from our hearts we abhor all sects of heresy, and all teachers of erroneous doctrine; and that with all humility we embrace the purity of Christ's Evangel, which is the only food of our souls; and therefore so precious unto us, that we are determined to suffer the extremity of worldly danger, rather than that we will suffer ourselves to be defrauded of the same. For we are most certainly persuaded, 'That whosoever denies Christ Jesus, or is ashamed of him, in presence of men, shall be denied before the Father, and before his holy angels.' And therefore by the assistance of the mighty Spirit of the same, our Lord Jesus, we firmly purpose to abide to the end in the Confession of this our Faith [as by the articles followed].

W. C. Dickinson (ed.), *John Knox's History of the Reformation in Scotland*, vol. II (1949), pp. 256–7.

During the crucial days of the Scottish Reformation, the Parliament of 1560 commissioned a small group of prominent rebel-ministers to produce a statement of their faith. Almost immediately, John Knox and his five associates complied with what came to be called the Scots Confession; and on 17 August 1560 Parliament adopted their production as 'wholesome and sound doctrine, grounded upon the infallible truth of God's Word'.

Though displaced in the following century by the much fuller and more systematic Westminster Confession, the earlier document is notable for its evangelical fervour (clearly evident in the phraseology of the Preface) and its claim to be Biblically based throughout – a claim which raises many questions in the minds of modern readers, but which in the sixteenth century commended it to all those who felt that the Roman Church of the day was substituting ecclesiastical traditions and pronouncements for the God-given authority of Holy Scripture. Many would still agree with one of the Confession's greatest admirers, Edward Irving, who said of it in the early nineteenth century that it was 'written in a most honest, straightforward, manly style, without compliment or flattery, without affectation of logical precision and learned accuracy, as if it came fresh from the heart of laborious workmen, all the day long busy with the preaching of the truth, and sitting down at night to embody the heads of what was continually taught'. And as late as the 1930s the great Continental theologian, Karl Barth, made the Scots Confession the basis of his influential Gifford Lectures in the University of Aberdeen.

※ ※ ※

MINISTER'S EXHORTATION BEFORE COMMUNION

Dearly beloved in the Lord, forasmuch as we be now assembled to cele-
brate the Holy Communion of the body and blood of our Saviour Christ,
let us consider these words of St. Paul, how he exhorted all persons diligently to try and examine themselves before they presume to eat of that
bread, and to drink of that cup; for as the benefit is great, if, with a true
penitent heart and lively faith, we receive that holy Sacrament (for then
we spiritually eat the flesh of Christ and drink His blood, then we dwell
in Christ and Christ in us, we be one with Christ, and Christ with us),
so is the danger great if we receive the same unworthily, for then we be
guilty of the body and blood of Christ our Saviour, we eat and drink
our own damnation, not considering the Lord's body, we kindle God's
wrath against us, and provoke Him to plague us with divers diseases
and sundry kinds of death.

And therefore, in the name and authority of the eternal God, and
of His Son Jesus Christ, I excommunicate from this Table all blasphemers of God, all idolaters, all adulterers, all that be in malice or envy, all
disobedient persons to father or mother, Princes or Magistrates, Pastors
or Preachers; all thieves and deceivers of their neighbours; and finally all
such as live a life fighting against the will of God: charging them, as they
will answer in the presence of Him who is the righteous Judge, that they
presume not to profane this most holy Table. And yet this I pronounce
not, to seclude any penitent person, how grievous soever his sins before
have been, so, that he feel in his heart unfeigned repentance for the
same; but only such as continue in sin without repentance. Neither yet is
this pronounced against such as aspire to a greater perfection than they
can in this present life attain unto; for, albeit we feel in ourselves much
frailty and wretchedness, as that we have not our faith so perfect and
constant as we ought, being many times ready to distrust God's goodness
through our corrupt nature; and also that we are not so thoroughly given
to serve God, neither have so fervent a zeal to set forth His glory, as our
duty requireth, feeling still such rebellion in ourselves, that we have need
daily to fight against the lusts of our flesh; yet nevertheless, seeing that
our Lord hath dealt thus mercifully with us, that He hath printed His
Gospel in our hearts, so that we are preserved from falling into despera-
tion and misbelief; and seeing also that He hath endued us with a will
and desire to renounce and withstand our own affections, with a longing
for His righteousness and the keeping of His commandments, we may be

now right well assured, that those defaults and manifold imperfections in us shall be no hindrance at all against us, to cause Him not to accept and impute us as worthy to come to His spiritual Table: for the end of our coming thither is not to make protestation that we are upright or just in our lives; but contrariwise, we come to seek our life and perfection in Jesus Christ, acknowledging in the meantime that we of ourselves be the children of wrath and damnation.

Let us consider, then, that this Sacrament is a singular medicine for all poor sick creatures, a comfortable help to weak souls, and that our Lord requireth no other worthiness on our part, but that we unfeignedly acknowledge our naughtiness and imperfection. Then, to the end that we may be worthy partakers of His merits, which is the true eating of His flesh and drinking of His blood, let us not suffer our minds to wander about the consideration of these earthly and corruptible things (which we see present to our eyes, and feel with our hands), to seek Christ present in them, as if He were enclosed in the bread and wine, as if these elements were turned and changed into the substance of His flesh and blood; for the only way to dispose our souls to receive nourishment, relief, and quickening of His substance, is to lift up our minds by faith above all things worldly and sensible, and thereby to enter into heaven, that we may find and receive Christ, where He dwelleth undoubtedly very God and very Man, in the incomprehensible glory of His Father, to whom be all praise, honour, and glory, now and forever. Amen.

From 'The Manner of the Administration of the Lord's Supper',
Book of Common Order (1564).

This eloquent exhortation to prospective communicants comes from the section entitled 'The Manner of the Administration of the Lord's Supper', which stands at the heart of the first service-book of the Reformed Church of Scotland, the *Book of Common Order* (1564). The words speak for themselves, but two observations must be made The first is that for conciseness and felicity of expression they lose little even when compared with the masterly profundity and succinctness of the corresponding service in Thomas Cranmer's English *Book of Common Prayer*; the second, that their dominant emphasis, most tenderly expressed, is not on the exclusion of the impenitent (though that is certainly there) but on the summons to penitent sinners to place their reliance on what is beautifully described as 'a singular medicine for all poor sick creatures'. The Sacrament of the Lord's Supper (to use the commonest description of the Eucharist in Reformed Scotland) was clearly the central, if not the most frequently celebrated act of worship – 'once a month, or so oft as the congregation shall think expedient' – from Knox's time onwards; and in this 'Exhortation' may be discerned the pastoral concern of Reformed churchmanship at its attractive best.

❧ ❧ ❧
A GODLIE PRAYER TO BE SAID
AT ALL TIMES

Honour and praise be given to thee, O Lord God Almighty, most dear
Father of heaven, for all Thy mercies and loving-kindness showed unto
us, in that it hath pleased Thy gracious goodness, freely and of Thine
own accord, to elect and choose us to salvation before the beginning of
the world; and even like continual thanks be given to Thee for creating
us after Thine own image; for redeeming us with the precious blood of
Thy dear Son, when we were utterly lost; for sanctifying us with Thy Holy
Spirit in the revelation and knowledge of Thy holy Word – for helping
and succouring us in all our needs and necessities – for saving us from
all dangers of body and soul – for comforting us so fatherly in all our
tribulations and persecutions – for sparing us so long, and giving us
so large a time of repentance. These benefits, O most merciful Father,
like as we acknowledge to have received them of Thine only goodness,
even so we beseech Thee, for Thy dear Son Jesus Christ's sake, to grant
us always Thy Holy Spirit, whereby we may continually grow in thankfulness towards Thee, to be led into all truth, and comforted in all our
adversities. O Lord, strengthen our faith, kindle it more in ferventness,
and love towards Thee, and our neighbours for Thy sake. Suffer us not,
most dear Father, to receive any more Thy word in vain, but grant us
always the assistance of Thy grace and Holy Spirit, that in heart, word,
and deed, we may sanctify and do worship to Thy name.

Help us to amplify and increase Thy kingdom, that whatsoever thou
sendest, we may be heartily well content with Thy good pleasure and
will. Let us not lack the thing, O Father, without the which we cannot
serve Thee; but bless Thou so all the work of our hands that we may have
sufficient, and not be chargeable but helpful unto others. Be merciful,
O Lord, to our offences; and seeing our debt is great, which Thou hast
forgiven us in Jesus Christ, make us to love Thee and our neighbours so
much the more. Be Thou our father, our Captain, and Defender in all
temptations; hold Thou us by Thy merciful hand, that we may be delivered from all inconveniences, and end our lives in the sanctifying and
honouring of Thy holy name, through Jesus Christ our Lord and only
Saviour. So be it.

Let Thy mighty hand and outstretched arm, O Lord, be still our
defence – Thy mercy and loving kindness in Jesus Christ, Thy dear Son,
our salvation – Thy true and holy Word our instruction – Thy grace and

Holy Spirit our comfort and consolation, unto the end and in the end.
So be it.

O Lord, increase our faith.

G. W. Sprott and T. Leishman (eds), *The Book of Common Order
and the Directory* (1868), pp. 231–2.

The sixteenth-century Reformers were careful not only to provide their fellow-ministers with guidance as to the conduct of public worship (the *Book of Common Order*), but also to supply heads of families with material for private devotions in the home. One of the instruments used to fashion the thinking of generations of Scottish children was an English translation of John Calvin's Geneva Catechism; and when it was published in the 1560s certain pattern prayers, conceivably the work of John Knox himself, were appended. This 'Godlie Prayer' was one of them. Formidably detailed (it might almost serve as a summary of Reformed theology), and despite its wordiness and heavily doctrinal content, it contains phrases – for example, 'Seeing our debt is great, which thou hast forgiven us in Jesus Christ, make us to love thee and our neighbours so much the more' – which come near to expressing the very heart of Christian piety in any age.

❧ ❧ ❧
PRAYER BEFORE WORK

O Lord God, most merciful Father and Saviour, seeing it hath pleased thee to command us to travail, that we may relieve our need, we beseech thee of thy grace so to bless our labour, that thy blessing may extend to us, without the which we are not able to continue, and that this great favour may be a witness unto us of thy bountifulness and assistance, so that thereby we may know the fatherly care that thou hast over us. Moreover, O Lord, we beseech thee, that thou wouldest strengthen us with thine Holy Spirit, that we may faithfully travail in our state and vocation without fraud or deceit; and that we may endeavour ourselves to follow thine holy ordinance, rather than to seek to satisfy our greedy affections or desire to gain. And if it please thee, O Lord, to prosper our labour, give us a mind also to help them that have need, according to that ability that thou of thy mercy shalt give us, and knowing that all good things come of thee, grant that we may humble ourselves to our neighbours, and not by any means lift ourselves up above them which have not received so liberal a portion, as of thy mercy thou hast given to us. And if it please thee to try and exercise us by greater poverty and need than our flesh would desire, that thou wouldst yet, O Lord, grant us grace to know that thou wilt nourish us continually through thy bountiful liberality, that we be not so tempted, that we fall into distrust; but that we may patiently wait till thou fill us, not only with corporal graces and benefits, but chiefly with thine heavenly and spiritual treasures, to the intent that we may always have more ample occasion to give thee thanks, and so wholly to rest upon thy mercies. Hear us, O Lord of mercy, through Jesus Christ thy Son our Lord. Amen.

D. Laing (ed.), Works of John Knox, vol. VI (1895), p. 360.

Much has been written in recent years about 'the Puritan work-ethic'. Here, in one of the prayers subjoined to the 1564 edition of Calvin's Geneva Catechism, is an attractive form of what could be a harshly self-regarding thing. 'Fraud or deceit' are denounced, along with 'greedy affections or desire to gain'; prosperity must issue in humble help for the needy; and if poverty comes, grace is sought 'that we be not so tempted that we fall into distrust: but that we may patiently wait till thou fill us, not only with corporal grace and benefits, but chiefly with thine heavenly and spiritual treasures'. How far such petitions affected the behaviour of those who used them must be answered from subsequent history – but at least the ideal was attractively presented to several generations of Scottish believers.

❦ ❦ ❦
SUMMONS TO WORSHIP

All people that on earth do dwell,
Sing to the Lord with cheerful voice.
Him serve with mirth, his praise forth tell,
Come ye before him and rejoice.

Know that the Lord is God indeed;
Without our aid he did us make;
We are his folk, he doth us feed,
And for his sheep he doth us take.

O enter then his gates with praise,
Approach with joy his courts unto;
Praise, laud, and bless his Name always,
For it is seemly so to do.

For why? The Lord our God is good,
His mercy is for ever sure;
His truth at all times firmly stood,
And shall from age to age endure.

Psalm 100, in *The Scottish Psalter* (1564).

The Old Testament Psalter, whether said or sung, has been at the heart of Christian worship since the earliest days of the Church; but it was only in the sixteenth century, and particularly during the Calvinist Reformation at Geneva, that *congregational singing* of the Psalms took over from recital by clergy or choirs. From Geneva's English-speaking congregation, with its many Scottish refugees, the custom of singing metrical versions of the Psalms was carried back to Scotland; and in 1564 John Knox and his associates had the complete Psalter – the Genevan version thoroughly revised – bound up with their service-book, the *Book of Common Order*. Every minister, elder and deacon was ordered by the General Assembly to possess a copy, and in course of time no family would be without one. In subsequent centuries, the words and music of the Psalter sang themselves into the hearts of innumerable Scots, and at their best they gave voice to some of the deepest and most passionate convictions of a whole people.

Among the translators of the Anglo-Genevan Psalter (to which he contributed 25 items) was William Kethe, most probably a Scot. From Geneva, where he seems to have had a hand in the production of the great Geneva Bible, beloved by Puritans and only gradually displaced by the Authorised Version of 1611, Keith retired to England, where he held various ecclesiastical appointments. But his lasting fame is due to his versification of the 100th Psalm, 'All people that on earth do dwell', which passed from the Anglo-Genevan Psalter to the 1564 Book and thence to the Scottish Psalter of 1650, and has continued to be sung ever since. Appropriately enough, it was the 100th Psalm in Kethe's translation which opened *The Church Hymnary* (3rd edn, 1973).

As celebrated as Kethe's words is Louis Bourgeois' noble tune, the 'Old Hundred'.

❦ ❦ ❦
GENERAL ASSEMBLY TO JOHN WILLOCK

Videbam Satanam sicut fulgur de Coelo cadentem

As the Lord our God hath at all times been from the beginning of this his work of Reformation and restitution of the purity of his true worship and religion within Scotland, (loving Brother in the Lord), most beneficial and bountiful towards this Realm, so hath he now by this last most miraculous victory and overthrow, poured forth in greatest abundance the riches of his mercy, in that not only he hath driven away the tempests and storm, but also hath quieted and calmed all surges of persecution; as now we may think well our ship is received, and placed in a most happy and pleasant port; our enemies, praised be God, are dashed, religion established; sufficient provision made for ministers; order taken, and penalties appointed, for all sorts of aggression and aggressors; and above all, a godly magistrate, whom God of his eternal and heavenly Providence hath reserved to this age, to put in execution whatsoever he by his law commandeth. Now then, loving Brother, as your presence was to us all in time of trouble most comfortable, so it is now of us all universally wished, but most earnestly craved by your own flock, who continually at all Assemblies have declared the force of that conjunction, the earnestness of that love, the pith of that zeal and mutual care that bindeth the Pastor with his flock, which neither by process of time is diminished, nor by separation and distance of place restricted, nor yet by tyranny and fear dissolved. True it is, that at this their most earnest and just petition, we have ever still winked this while bypast; not but that to us all your absence was most dolorous; but in respect of troubles, we judged more meet to await for such opportunity as now God, in this most wonderful victory of his Evangel, hath offered.

Therefore seeing all impediments are removed, and your flock still continueth in earnest suit for you, and now everywhere throughout the Realm Commissioners and Superintendents placed, and one offered to them, and by them refused altogether, awaiting for you; we could no longer stay, but agree to this their desire, in suit whereof neither through fear have they fainted, nor by charges retarded, nor yet by any kind of offer desisted; and as we have been moved to grant to them that which they have thus humbly and continually suited, we cannot but persuade ourselves but you will satisfy the same; neither can we think that the shepherd will refuse his flock; that the father will reject the just petition of his son; least of all, that the faithful servant of God will shut up his ears at the voice and commandment of the Kirk, or yet deny his labours to his own Country. The time is proper now to reap with blitheness that which by you before was sown in tears, and enjoy the fruit of your most wearisome and painful labours. It shall be no less pleasant to you to see your own native Country at liberty and freedom, which ye left mourning and sobbing, under the heavy burden of most cruel servitude, than comfortable to behold the religion of Jesus Christ throughout all the Realm flourishing, virtue increasing, virtuous men in reputation; and finally to embrace these days, which howsoever by yourself they have been most piously desired, yet could you never look to attain the same. Now, at last, to conclude, unless you will be an enemy to your Country, you will not refuse these requests; unless you will be stubborn and disobedient, you will not contemn the commandment of the Kirk; unless you be careless and unthankful, you will not despise the humble, continual and earnest suit of your flock; and last of all we assure ourselves, that you are not so astricted and addicted to your own particular, as that this general and common cause should be in any wise by you neglected. Now you shall see the copestone of that Work whereof you laid the foundation. Thus we cannot look for any other answer than you shall give by yourself, and with all expedition possible. Our state, you know, is not so sure but we ever stand upon our watches; but that, we know, will not stay you, seeing your account is so laid. Thus we commit you to the protection of our Lord Jesus. At Edinburgh, in our GENERAL ASSEMBLY, and seventh Session thereof (January 1567–8).

D. Laing (ed.), *The Works of John Knox*, vol. VI (1895), pp. 445–6.

This letter, written on behalf of the General Assembly shortly after Queen Mary's enforced abdication in 1567, begins by expressing the elation felt by Knox and his associates at a remarkable up-turn in their fortunes: 'Our enemies, praised be God, are dashed . . .'. Scotland now had a Protestant King (the infant James VI), together with what later ages would describe as a Protestant Establishment. Much, however, remained to be done, as was demonstrated, soon after Knox wrote, by the outbreak of a six-year-long civil war; and at this turning-point in the struggle for Reformation the Assembly's thoughts inevitably turned to their fundamental and overriding concern – the well-being of the parishes, the local religious communities of Scotland. Not the cathedral or the monastery but the parish kirk was the key to national rejuvenation; and so recruitment of worthy pastors and preachers was clearly the top priority.

None more worthy was to be found than John Willock. He may well have been the leading figure in the reform movement in the years before Knox returned to Scotland in 1559; and the esteem in which he was held is indicated by his appointment as Superintendent of Glasgow in the immediate aftermath of the religious revolution, as well as by the five occasions on which he was called to be Moderator of the General Assembly between 1563 and 1568. The urgency of this letter underlines his importance, and it may be presumed to have brought about his return to Scotland soon after he received it – though, despite all contrary pressures, it did not induce him to remain for more than a few months. Even more significant, however, is the implication, clearly evident in the letter, that the overriding authority in the new order was the local congregation, whose call dared not be refused: 'unless you will be stubborn and disobedient, you will not contemn the commandment of the Kirk; unless you will be careless and unthankful you will not despise the humble, continual and earnest suit of your flock'. It would be difficult to find a more striking testimony to the centrality of the parish ministry, and to the bond between minister and people which has been an ever-recurrent feature of Reformed experience over five centuries.

✷ ✷ ✷

SONG OF DELIVERANCE

Now Israel may say, and that truly,
If that the Lord had not our cause maintained;
If that the Lord had not our cause sustained,
When cruel men against us furiously
Rose up in wrath to make of us their prey;

Then certainly they had devoured us all,
And swallowed quick, for aught that we could deem;
Such was their rage, as we might well esteem.
And as fierce floods before them all things drown,
So had they brought our souls to death quite down.

The raging streams, with their proud swelling waves,
Had then our soul overwhelmed in the deep.
But blest be God, who doth us safely keep,
And hath not given us for a living prey
Unto their teeth, and bloody cruelty.

Even as a bird out of the fowler's snare
Escapes away, so is our soul set free;
Broke are their nets, and thus escaped we.
Therefore our help is in the Lord's great Name,
Who heaven and earth by his great power did frame.

Psalm 124, in *The Scottish Psalter* (1564).

Metrical psalm-singing, which was originally imported from Calvin's Geneva, quickly became one of the most valued features of religious life in late sixteenth-century Scotland. James Melville, nephew of the outstanding Presbyterian leader in the generation after Knox, Andrew Melville, writes as follows about the introduction of the practice in the area surrounding the town of Montrose: 'The laird of Dun of his charity entertained a blind man, who had a singularly good voice; him he caused the doctor of the school teach the whole Psalms in metre, with the tunes thereof, and sing them in the kirk; by hearing of whom I was so delighted that I learnt many of the psalms and tunes thereof in metre, which I have thought ever since a great blessing and comfort.'

Of these psalms, 'Now Israel may say', William Whittingham's version of Psalm 124, seems to have been a special favourite. David Calderwood the historian gives a memorable account of how, as early as 1582, a popular preacher of the time, John Durie, was welcomed back to Edinburgh by a psalm-singing crowd of its inhabitants: 'At the Netherbow they took up the 124 Psalm, "Now Israel may say", etc., and sung in such a pleasant tune in four parts, known to the most part of the people, that coming up the street all bare-headed till they entered in the kirk (St Giles'), with such a great sound and majestic, that it moved both themselves and all the huge multitude of the beholders, looking out at the shots and over stairs, with admiration and astonishment.' More than three centuries later, the victory of 1945 was celebrated in churches throughout Scotland by the singing of this same 124th Psalm.

Whittingham contributed several translations of the Psalms, including this one, to the Genevan Psalter and, subsequently, to the 1564 Book sponsored by Knox and his reforming colleagues. He was for a short time Knox's successor as minister of the Anglo-Scottish congregation of refugees in Geneva, and deserves honourable mention as one of the translators of the hugely influential Geneva Bible. He returned from the Continent to Elizabeth's England, and ended a stormy career as Dean of Durham.

Seventeenth Century

*** *** ***
# THE NATIONAL COVENANT

From the knowledge and consciences of our duty to God, to our King and Country, without any worldly respect and inducement, so far as human infirmity will suffer, wishing a further measure of the grace of God for this effect, We promise and swear by the Great Name of the Lord our God to continue in the Profession and Obedience of the foresaid (Reformed) Religion. That we shall defend the same, and resist all these contrary errours and corruptions, according to our vocation, and to the uttermost of that power that God hath put in our hands, all the days of our life . . . And because we cannot look for a blessing from God upon our proceedings, except with our Profession and Subscription we join such a life and conversation, as beseemeth Christians, who have renewed their Covenant with God; we, therefore, faithfully promise, for ourselves, our followers, and all other under us, both in publick, in our particular families, and personal carriage, to endeavour to keep ourselves within the bounds of Christian liberty, and to be good examples to others of all Godlinesse, Sobernesse, and Righteousnesse, and of every duty we owe to God and Man, And that this our Union and Conjunction may be observed without violation, we call the living God, the Searcher of our Hearts to witness, who knoweth this to be our sincere Desire, and unfeigned Resolution, as we shall answer to Jesus Christ, in the great day, and under the pain of God's everlasting wrath, and of infamy, and losse of all honour and respect in this World, most humbly beseeching the Lord to strengthen us by his holy Spirit for this end, and to bless our desires and proceedings with a happy successe, that Religion and Righteousnesse may flourish in the Land, to the glory of God, the honour of our King, and peace and comfort of us all. In witness whereof we have subscribed with our hands all the premises, etc.

W. C. Dickinson and G. Donaldson, Source Book of Scottish History
(1954), vol. III, pp. 102–4.

The National Covenant of 1638, was essentially an appeal to the Scottish people against the policies, political and religious, of Charles I's government, and in particular the imposition on the country, without submission to either Parliament or General Assembly, of deeply unwelcome worship practices which were believed to lead back to some of the worst excesses of pre-Reformation churchmanship. Its principal authors were Alexander Henderson, successively minister of Leuchars, Greyfriars and St Giles', Edinburgh, once described as 'incomparably the ablest man of us all for all things', and Archibald Johnston of Wariston, a formidably learned lawyer whose ardent piety was not always distinguishable from mania. Signed initially in Greyfriars Kirk, the Covenant was distributed throughout the land, and became the object of fervent devotion. Within months, it took the 'Covenanters' to war with the King; but more than half a century was to elapse before their major contentions were finally enshrined in the Revolution Settlement of 1690.

Nowhere has historical revisionism been more active than in the treatment of the Covenant and Covenanters. The most concise twentieth-century account is David Stevenson's Saltire pamphlet, *The Covenanters: The National Covenant and Scotland* (1988); a traditional Presbyterian version may be found, at great length, in J. K. Hewison's massive two-volume study from the first decade of the twentieth century, *The Covenanters*.

The closing paragraphs of the Covenant (reproduced here) express the profoundly religious convictions which were subsequently overlaid by less attractive features of popular piety.

❊ ❊ ❊
THE CHRISTIAN'S LIFE:
A MIXTURE OF GOOD AND EVIL

There are few or none of the children of God in whom something may not be marked which tends to infirmity, and there be few or none of them in whom something may not be marked; and I may say more, who of them is there in whom God has not marked many things? Before the spirit of regeneration come, and we are in nature, then are we wholly in darkness and ill, and when we are in glory then we are altogether good and in light; but while we are here into the state of grace there is a mixture of good and ill in us, of light and darkness. And if so be it be true grace we have, we will see it to be so, and if it be true grace then that which is imperfect will be passed by and that which is good will be remembered. And this woman [Sarah] she made a lie yet that is passed by in silence, and only her faith is remembered; and the Spirit of God speaking in Job says, 'Ye have heard of the patience of Job', yet there was much impatience in him, but there is no word of that. And all the saints of God while they are here have many infirmities and yet the Lord passes by all these and remembers only of that which is good in them. The Lord He is glad to put down his hand and gather up the smallest crumbs of faith and make something of them; and not only does He this with Abraham or Moses or such worthies as these; but even Sarah He remembers her faith, and Rahab's, and passes by all their ill – never a word of that. It is not so much as mentioned of some of them that there was such a thing. Yet this is a matter of great comfort to the children of God who sees all their best actions to be greatly stained with infirmity, so as they think they rather deserve to be punished for their unbelief than to be rewarded for their faith. But this may comfort us if so be that our faith be true and sincere, albeit it be but weak, yet the Lord will accept that weak faith and will respect it, especially when it is unfeigned and it is a wise faith and there is a desire to have it increased.

From a sermon by Alexander Henderson, in R. L. Orr, *Alexander Henderson, Churchman and Statesman* (1919), pp. 393–4.

E ulogies seem to come easily in any discussion of Alexander Henderson (1583–1646). Described by a contemporary as 'the ablest man of us all for all things', and by a Victorian authority (David Masson) as 'the greatest, wisest, and most liberal of the Scottish Presbyterians', he rose to eminence during the Covenanting crisis of the late sixteen-thirties. While minister at Leuchars, in Fife, he petitioned the Privy Council against the unpopular Service-Book imposed on the Kirk by royal and episcopal authority, and in consequence was called successively to the leading charges of Greyfriars and St Giles' in Edinburgh. Joint author of the National Covenant and Moderator of the revolutionary General Assembly of November, 1638, he led Scotland's commissioners from 1643 onwards to the Westminster Assembly of Divines. His last months were spent in fruitless negotiations with the King.

Though his life ended in apparent failure, Henderson was indubitably a great man, eloquent, judicious and brave, with a balanced and charitable disposition which marked him off both from his sovereign and at least some of his Covenanting colleagues. The tenderness and deep faith of which he was capable are clearly revealed in this passage from one of his sermons.

❦ ❦ ❦
A RHAPSODICAL MEDITATION

There is not a rose out of heaven, but there is a blot and thorn growing out of it, except that one only rose of Sharon, which blossometh out glory. Every leaf of that rose is a heaven, and serveth 'for the healing of the nations'; every white and red in it, is incomparable glory; every act of breathing out its smell, from everlasting to everlasting, is spotless and unmixed happiness. Christ is the outset, the master-flower, the uncreated garland of heaven, the love and joy of men and angels. But the fountain-love, the fountain-delight, the fountain-joy of men and angels is more. For out of it flow all the seas, springs, rivers and floods of love, delight and joy. Christ cannot tire or weary from eternity to be Christ; and so, he must not, he cannot but be an infinite and eternal flowing sea, to diffuse and let out streams and floods of boundless grace. Say that the rose were eternal; the sweet smell, the loveliness of greenness and colour must be eternal. Oh, what a happiness, for a soul to lose its excellency in His transcendent glory! What a blessedness for the creature, to cast in his little all, in Christ's matchless self-sufficiency! Could all the streams retire into the fountain and first spring, they should be kept in a more sweet and firm possession of their being, in the bosom of their first cause, than in their borrowed channels that they now move in. Our neighbourhood, and retiring in, to dwell for ever and ever in the fountain-blessedness, Jesus Christ, with our borrowed goodness, is the firm and solid fruition of our eternal happy being. Christ is the sphere, the con-natural first spring and element of borrowed drops and small pieces of created grace. The rose is surest in being, in beauty, on its own stock and root: let life and sap be eternally in the stock and root, and the rose keep its first union with the root, and it shall never wither, never cast its blossom nor greenness of beauty. It is violence for a gracious soul to be out of his stalk and root; union here is life and happiness; therefore the Church's last prayer in canonic Scripture is for union, 'Amen: even so, come Lord Jesus.' It shall not be well till the Father and Christ the prime heir, and all the weeping children, be under one roof in the palace royal. It is a sort of mystical lameness, that the head wanteth an arm or a finger; and it is a violent and forced condition, for arm and finger to be separated from the head. The saints are little pieces of mystical Christ, sick of love for union. The wife of youth, that wants her husband some years, and expects he shall return to her from over-sea lands, is often on the shore; every ship coming near shore is her new joy; her heart loves the wind that shall bring him home. She asks at every passenger news: 'Oh! Saw ye my husband? What is he doing? When shall he come? Is he shipped for a return?' Every ship that carrieth not her husband, is the breaking of her heart. The bride, the Lamb's wife, blesseth the feet of the messengers that preach such tidings, 'Rejoice, O Zion, put on thy beautiful garments, thy King is coming.' Yea, she loveth that quarter of the sky, that being rent asunder and cloven, shall yield to her Husband, when he shall put through his glorious hand, and shall come riding on the rainbow and clouds to receive her to himself.

Samuel Rutherford, Trial and Triumph of Faith (1645), dedication,
in The Evangelical Succession (1883), pp. 169–71.

This highly-charged passage from the dedication to a volume of his sermons was written, not by a cloistered ascetic such as Bernard of Clairvaux or Theresa of Avila but by a Scottish Puritan of Covenanting times. Samuel Rutherford (1600–61) is not a character who immediately attracts the modern mind; but the story of his life, his accomplishments, and his extraordinarily diverse gifts cannot but impress. Minister at Anwoth, in Galloway, from 1627 to 1636, where (it was said) he 'seemed to be always praying, always preaching, always visiting the sick, always catechising, always writing and studying'; exiled to Aberdeen (1636–8) for his courageous opposition to royal policies; Professor of Divinity and later Principal of St Mary's College, St Andrews, after the triumph of the Covenanting opposition in 1638; commissioner to the Westminster Assembly of Divines from 1644 to 1648; awesome controversialist, especially in the sixteen-forties and fifties, and author of numerous incredibly learned treatises – including the classic *Lex Rex* – against Royalists, Episcopalians, Antinomians, Arminians, Independents, and even the more moderate Resolutioners within the Covenanting ranks; scholastic theologian and passionate preacher; legalist and mystic whose pastoral letters, commended by his near-contemporary Richard Baxter ('Hold off the Bible, such a book as Mr. Rutherfurd's Letters the world never saw the like'), were the favourite reading of many devout Victorian Scots: he defies categorisation. But perhaps the most informative and discerning account of him is to be found in a lecture by the Edinburgh lawyer, Alexander Taylor Innes, which was published with others in 1883 under the title, *The Evangelical Succession*. From it this extract is taken.

THE WESTMINSTER DIVINES ON PREACHING

Preaching of the word, being the power of God unto salvation, and one of the greatest and most excellent works belonging to the ministry of the gospel, should be so performed, that the workman need not be ashamed, but may save himself, and those that hear him.

It is presupposed (according to the rules for ordination), that the minister of Christ is in some good measure gifted for so weighty a service, by his skill in the original languages, and in such arts and sciences as are handmaid unto divinity; by his knowledge in the whole body of theology, but most of all in the holy scriptures, having his senses and heart exercised in them above the common sort of believers; and by the illumination of God's Spirit, and other gifts of edification, which (together with reading and studying of the word) he ought still to seek by prayer, and an humble heart, resolving to admit and receive any truth not yet attained, whenever God shall make it known to him. All which he is to make use of, and improve, in his private preparations, before he deliver in public what he hath provided.

Ordinarily, the subject of his sermon is to be some text of Scripture, holding forth some principle or head of religion, or suitable to some special occasion emergent; or he may go on in some chapter, psalm, or book of the holy scripture, as he shall think fit . . .

But the servant of God, whatever his method be, is to perform his whole ministry:

1. Painfully, not doing the work of the Lord negligently.

2. Plainly, that the meanest may understand; delivering the truth not in the enticing words of man's wisdom, but in demonstration of the Spirit and of power, lest the cross of Christ should be made of none effect; abstaining also from an unprofitable use of unknown tongues, strange phrases, and cadences of sounds and words, sparingly citing sentences of ecclesiastical or other human writers, ancient or modern, be they never so elegant.

3. Faithfully, looking at the honour of Christ, the conversion, education, and salvation of the people, not at his own gain or glory, keeping nothing back which may promote those holy ends, giving to everyone his own portion, and bearing indifferent respect unto all, without neglecting the meanest, or sparing the greatest, in their sins.

4. Wisely, framing all his doctrines, exhortations, and especially his reproofs, in such a manner as may be most likely to prevail, showing all due respect to each man's person and place, and not mixing his own passion or bitterness.

5. Gravely, as becometh the word of God; shunning all such gesture, voice, and expressions, as may occasion the corruptions of men to despise him and his ministry.

6. With loving affection, that the people may see all coming from his godly zeal, and hearty desire to do them good. And

7. As taught of God, and persuaded in his own heart, that all he teaches is the truth of Christ, and walking before his flock, as an example to them in it; earnestly, both in private and publick, recommending his labours to the blessing of God, and watchfully looking to himself, and the flock whereof the Lord hath made him overseer. So shall the doctrine of truth be preserved uncorrupt, many souls converted and built up, and himself receive manifold comforts of his labours even in this life, and afterward the crown of glory laid up for him in the world to come.

Westminster Directory for the Public Worship of God (1645).

There is no denying the centrality of preaching in the Scottish Presbyterian tradition. The proclamation of the Faith, on the basis of the Biblical witness, has from the Reformation onwards been at the heart of worship in Scotland. It was above all by preaching that the country was translated into a new era, with new ideals and new priorities, by Patrick Hamilton, George Wishart, John Knox and the other reformers; and when the Westminster Divines, a century later, set about fashioning a truly 'godly' Church they inevitably devoted much attention to the definition and commendation of preaching. These lapidary sentences from their *Book of Common Order* convey a sense of their confidence that, if properly exercised, the preaching of the Word would indeed bring new life to the Church. With all its failures, the Kirk of succeeding centuries has not altogether disappointed their expectations.

✸ ✸ ✸
A BORDER CONVENTICLE

The place where we convened was in every way commodious, and seemed to have been formed on purpose. It was a green and pleasant haugh, fast by the waterside [the Whitadder]. In both directions there was a spacious brae, in form of a half-round, covered with delightful pasture, and rising with a gentle slope to a goodly height. Above us was the clear blue sky, for it was a sweet and calm Sabbath morning . . . The Communion Tables were spread on the green by the water; and around them the people had arranged themselves in decent order. But far the greater multitude sat on the brae-face, which was crowded from top to bottom. The Tables were served by some gentlemen, persons of the gravest deportment. None were admitted without tokens as usual, which were distributed on the Saturday, but only to such as were known to the ministers . . . All the regular forms were gone through; the communicants entered at one end, and retired at the other, the way being kept clear for them to take their seats again on the hillside. Mr. Welsh preached the action sermon, and served the first two tables; the other four ministers, Mr. Blackadder, Mr. Dickson, Mr. Riddel and Mr. Rae, exhorted the rest in turn. The Table services were closed by Mr. Welsh, with solemn thanksgiving. The communion was peaceably concluded, all the people heartily offering up their gratitude, and singing with a joyful noise to the Rock of their salvation. It was pleasant as night fell to hear their melody swelling in full unison along the hills. About 100 sat at every Table; there were 16 Tables served, so that about 3,200 communicated that day. The afternoon sermon was preached by Mr. Dickson, and the season of solemn services was brought to a close with a sermon on Monday afternoon by Mr. Blackadder.

John Blackadder, *Memoirs* (1823).

John Blackadder the elder (1615–86) was 'extruded' (i.e. removed) from his parish of Troqueer, near Dumfries, soon after the monarchical and episcopal Restoration of 1662, and became a conventicling preacher. Outlawed and hunted throughout the Border region, he fled for a time to the Netherlands. Returning soon after, he was condemned to house arrest in Edinburgh and eventually banished to the Bass Rock, where he died. His son, John Blackadder the younger, became an officer in the post-Revolution Cameronian regiment, in which he had a distinguished career.

John Blackadder senior's account of a Border conventicle may be somewhat lidealised; but it nevertheless gives an impressive picture of what the larger gatherings of Covenanters must have been like.

♀ ♀ ♀
THE DIVINE SHEPHERD

The Lord's my shepherd, I'll not want,
　　He makes me down to lie
In pastures green: he leadeth me
　　The quiet waters by.

My soul he doth restore again;
　　And me to walk doth make
Within the paths of righteousness,
　　Even for his own name's sake.

Yea, though I walk in death's dark vale,
　　Yet will I fear none ill:
For thou art with me; and thy rod
　　And staff me comfort still.

My table thou hast furnishèd
　　In presence of my foes;
My head thou dost with oil anoint,
　　And my cup overflows.

Goodness and mercy all my life
　　Shall surely follow me:
And in God's house for evermore
　　My dwelling-place shall be.

Psalm 23, in Scottish Metrical Psalter (1650).

❋ ❋ ❋
PRAISE FOR THE DIVINE MERCIES

O Thou my soul, bless God the Lord;
   And all that in me is
Be stirred up his holy Name
   To magnify and bless.

Bless, O my soul, the Lord thy God,
   And not forgetful be
Of all his gracious benefits
   He hath bestowed on thee.

All thine iniquities who doth
   most graciously forgive:
Who thy diseases all and pains
   Doth heal, and thee relieve.

Who doth redeem thy life, that thou
   To death may'st not go down;
Who thee with loving-kindness doth
   And tender mercies crown.

Who with abundance of good things
   Doth satisfy thy mouth;
So that, ev'n as the eagle's age,
   Renewed is thy youth.

O bless the Lord, all ye his works,
   Wherewith the world is stored
In his dominions everywhere,
   My soul, bless thou the Lord.

Psalm 103:1–5, 22, in Scottish Metrical Psalter (1650).

✻ ✻ ✻

TRUST IN THE DIVINE GUARDIANSHIP

I to the hills will lift mine eyes,
　From whence doth come mine aid.
My safety cometh from the Lord,
　Who heaven and earth hath made.

Thy foot he'll not let slide, nor will
　He slumber that thee keeps.
Behold, he that keeps Israel,
　He slumbers not, nor sleeps.

The Lord thee keeps, the Lord thy shade
　On thy right hand doth stay;
The moon by night thee shall not smite,
　Nor yet the sun by day.

The Lord shall keep thy soul; he shall
　Preserve thee from all ill.
Henceforth thy going out and in
　God keep for ever will.

Psalm 121, in Scottish Metrical Psalter (1650).

As noted earlier, the Scottish Psalter of the 1560s introduced Knox's contemporaries to what quickly established itself as the characteristic expression of the new faith; and it is worth remembering that its contents – in all their rugged and sometimes crude simplicity – were not only the sole opportunity for congregations to take an audible (and prescribed) part in Sabbath worship, but were also frequently employed, from Reformation times on, in regular family devotions. It was, however, the much-revised of 1635/1650 (to which Scottish churchmen made a very substantial contribution) that came to be the most long-lasting and best-loved version of the Hebrew original; and from the mid-seventeenth century to the present day has occupied an altogether special place in the affections of the Scottish people.

Their influence was never greater than in early Victorian times, as may be realised from the enthusiastic tribute paid by a learned Free Church minister, Norman Livingston, in 1864. He wrote:

> These verses, were interwoven with the religious being of the people, and formed the wings on which their pious feelings arose in wail or triumph to heaven. How sedulously were they conned in childhood! How emulously recited in the school and the family! How vividly recalled in seasons of danger and sorrow! How fondly quoted on the bed of sickness and death! How indelibly were they associated with critical emergencies, signal deliverances, seasons of revival, and other memorable occasions in the history of the Church! How largely did they minister to religious enjoyment and the progress of spiritual life in individual souls, as sung from day to day in the family, and from Sabbath to Sabbath in the sanctuary! Who can tell how much they contributed to the formation of that national character which, based on Bible knowledge and surmounted by pious fervour, contended so successfully with superstition and tyranny, and stamped its impress so deeply upon succeeding generations!
>
> N. Livingston, *The Scottish Metrical Psalter of 1635, with Tunes* (1864).

❀ ❀ ❀
A UNIVERSITY EXHORTATION

Would you have me speak the truth with freedom and brevity? The whole world is a kind of stage, and its inhabitants mere actors. As to this little farce of yours, it is now very near a conclusion, and you are upon the point of applying to the spectators for their applause. Should any superciliously decline paying his small tribute, you surely may, with great ease, retort their contempt upon themselves, merely by saying, 'Let your severity fall heavy on those who admire their own performances; as to this affair of ours, we know it is nothing at all': for I will not allow myself to doubt that you are very sensible, that there is indeed nothing in it . . .

As for you, young gentlemen, especially those of you that intend to devote yourselves to theological studies, it is my earnest advice and request to you, that you fly far from that infectious curiosity which would lead you into the depths of that controversial, contentious theology which, if any doctrine at all deserves the name, may be truly termed, 'science falsely so called'. And that you may not, in this respect, be imposed upon by the common reputation of acuteness and learning, I confidently affirm, that, to understand and be master of those trifling disputes that prevail in the schools, is an evidence of a very mean understanding; while, on the contrary, it is an argument of a genius truly great, entirely to slight and despise them, and to walk in the light of pure and peaceable truth, which is far above the dark and cloudy region of controversial disputes. But, you will say, it is necessary, in order to the defence of truth, to oppose errors, and blunt the weapons of sophists. Be it so; but our disputes ought to be managed with few words, for naked truth is most effectual for its own defence: and when it is once well understood, its natural light dispels all the darkness of error; 'for all things that are reproved, are made manifest by the light', saith the apostle . . .

There is but one useful controversy and dispute, one sort of war, most noble in its nature, or most worthy of a Christian, and this not to be carried on against enemies at a great distance, but such as are bred within our own breasts; against those it is most reasonable to wage an endless war, and these it is our duty to persecute to death. Let us all, children, young men and old, exert ourselves vigorously in this warfare; let our vices die before us, that death may not find us indolent, defiled, and wallowing in the mire; for then it will be most truly, and to our great misery, death to us; whereas, to those sanctified souls, who are conformed to Christ, and conquerors by his means, it rather is to be called life, as it delivers them from their wanderings and vices, from all kinds of evils, and from that death which is final and eternal.

The Works of Robert Leighton, D.D., Archbishop of Glasgow (1860),
pp. 623–4.

❧ ❧ ❧
A UNIVERSITY PRAYER

Most exalted God, who hast alone created, and dost govern this whole frame, and all the inhabitants thereof, visible and invisible, whose name alone is wonderful, and to be celebrated with the highest praise, as it is indeed above all praise and admiration. Let the heavens, the earth, and all the elements praise thee; let darkness, light, and all the returns of days and years, and all the varieties and vicissitudes of things, praise thee; let the angels praise thee, the archangels, and all the blessed court of heaven, whose very happinesss it is, that they are constantly employed in celebrating thy praises. We confess, O Lord, that we are of all creatures the most unworthy to praise thee; yet, of all others, we are under the greatest obligations to do it; nay, the more unworthy we are, our obligation is so much the greater. From this duty, however unqualified we may be, we can by no means abstain, nor indeed ought we. Let our souls bless thee, and all that is within us praise thy holy name, who forgivest all our sins, and healest all our diseases, who deliverest our souls from destruction, and crownest them with bounty and tender mercies. Thou searchest the heart, O Lord, and perfectly knowest the most intimate recesses of it: reject not those prayers which thou perceives to be the voice and wishes of the heart: now it is the great request of our hearts, unless they always deceive us, that they may be weaned from all earthly and perishing enjoyments; and if there is anything to which they cleave with more than ordinary force, may they be pulled away from it by thy Almighty hand, that they may be joined to thee for ever in an inseparable marriage-covenant; and, in our behalf, we have nothing more to ask. We only add, in behalf of thy church, that it may be protected under the shadow of thy wings, and everywhere, throughout the world, watered by thy heavenly dew, that the spirit and heat of worldly hatred against it may be cooled, and its intestine divisions, whereby it is much more grievously scorched, extinguished. Bless this nation, this city, and this university, in which we beg thou wouldst be pleased to reside, as in a garden dedicated to thy name, through Jesus Christ our Lord. Amen.

From 'Exhortations to the Candidates for the Degree of Master of Arts in the University of Edinburgh', *The Works of Robert Leighton, D.D., Archbishop of Glasgow* (1860), pp. 622–3.

R obert Leighton (1611–84), minister of Newbattle in the 1640s, and signatory of the Solemn League and Covenant in 1643 (though he later deplored the intolerance with which it came to be associated), was appointed Principal of Edinburgh University in 1653. After the Restoration, he became Bishop of Dunblane, and Archbishop of Glasgow in 1670. An eirenic spirit in a highly contentious age, he strove hard, but in vain, for reconciliation with those Presbyterians who rejected the church settlement effected in 1660 and subsequently. Thwarted and disheartened, he resigned his see in 1674 and retired to England, shortly after writing of Scotland's 'unworthy and trifling contentions' as 'a drunken scuffle in the dark'. He has had many admirers, of whom the Latitudinarian Bishop Burnet of Salisbury was one of the earliest. S. T. Coleridge based his *Aids to Reflection* on some of Leighton's sayings, and modern ecumenists see in him a happy blend of Episcopalian and Presbyterian insights.

Eighteenth
Century

✵ ✵ ✵
COVENANT RENEWAL

Lord, if I have done iniquity, I am resolved by Thy grace to do so no more. I flee for shelter to the blood of Jesus and His everlasting right-eousness; for this is pleasing unto Thee. I offer myself up, soul and body, unto God the Father, Son and Holy Ghost. I offer myself unto Christ the Lord, as an object proper for all His offices to be exercised upon. I choose Him as my Prophet, for instruction, illumination and direction. I embrace Him as my great Priest, to be washed and justified by His blood and righteousness. I embrace Him as my King, to reign and rule within me. I take a whole Christ, with all His laws, and all His crosses and afflictions. I except against none of them. I will live to Him; I will die to Him; I will quit with all I have in the world for His cause and truth. Only, Thou must be surety for me, and fulfil in me all the good pleasure of Thy goodness. Thou must fulfil both Thy own part and my part of this covenant; for this is the tenor of Thy covenant, 'I will be their God, and they shall be my people; I will put my Spirit within them, and cause them to walk in my statutes; when thou passest through the waters I will be with thee; I will never, never leave thee nor forsake thee.' Lord, upon these terms, I renew my covenant this night; and I take heaven and earth, angels and men, sun and moon and stars, the stones and timber of this house, to witness, that upon these terms, I give myself away, in soul and body and estate, and all I am or have in this world, unto God, Father, Son and Holy Ghost. And upon these terms I subscribe myself – Thy sworn servant forever.

Ebenezer Erskine (c.1708/09),
in A. R. MacEwen, *The Erskines* (1900), p. 33.

A lthough the political epoch of the Covenants may be said to have ended
when no mention was made of them in the Revolution Settlement of
1690, 'covenanting' as a personal religious exercise continued well into the
eighteenth century among staunchly Evangelical ministers and their flocks.
Nowhere was it more deep-rooted than in the leaders and followers of the
Secession of 1733, whose piety, modelled not only upon the spirit and
phraseology of the National Covenant of 1638 but on various covenants in
Scottish history as far back as the days of Knox, claimed an ancestry which
extended into Old Testament times.

Ebenezer Erskine (1680–1754), the father of the Secession, ministered
at Portmoak (near Loch Leven) and then in Stirling, and became a leader of
those devout traditionalists in the Kirk who deplored the backsliding of men
soon to become the vanguard of 'enlightened' Moderatism. Clashing with
the General Assembly over its operation of patronage and its refusal to listen
to the voice of congregations in ministerial settlements, he helped to form
an 'associate' (semi-detached) presbytery of the Church in 1733, and was
formally deposed from his charge in 1740. Before he died, several thousands
of evangelically-minded Scots had joined him in the Secession Church, and
by the end of the century Dissenting Presbyterianism was an influential force
in Scottish Christianity.

❦ ❦ ❦
'SMOKING SPIRITUALISED'

Was this small plant for thee cut down?
So was the plant of great renown,
Which mercy sends
For nobler ends:
Thus think, and smoke tobacco.

Doth juice medicinal proceed
From such a naughty, foreign weed?
Then what's the power
Of Jesse's flower?
Thus think, and smoke tobacco.

The promise, like the pipe, inlays
And by the mouth of faith conveys
What virtue flows
From Sharon's Rose:
Thus think, and smoke tobacco.

In vain the unlighted pipe you blow;
Your pains in outward means are so,
Till heavenly fire
Your heart inspire:
Thus think, and smoke tobacco.

The smoke, like burning incense, towers;
So should a praying heart of yours
With ardent cries
Surmount the skies:
Thus think, and smoke tobacco.

Ralph Erskine, in A. R. MacEwen, *The Erskines* (1900), p. 47.

Ralph Erskine (1685–1752), brother of the even more celebrated Ebenezer, ministered at Dunfermline from 1711 until his death. After enduring agonies of doubt and hesitation, he joined his seceding brother in 1737, and became a leader of the infant Secession Church, famous not only for his preaching but his poetry (*Scripture Songs*, 1754, and *Gospel Sonnets*, 25th edn, 1797). In the rather unsympathetic 1920s one of his biographers, J. H. Leckie, wrote that: 'It is to Ralph Erskine's credit that he retained in those direful days the ability to write verse at all, and that he found leisure to exercise it in the midst of such a toiling life. It may be admitted, too, that there seems to have been magnetic power in the man who could educe even a trickle of poetry from the hard rock of high Calvinistic dogma.'

'Smoking Spiritualised' – a kind of Seceding *jeu d'esprit* – may be seen as evidence of a concern for the Christianisation of absolutely every human activity, smoking included; but its didacticism is lightened by what could almost be called playfulness. To quote Leckie again, 'There was a streak of genius and much sound and warm humanity, as well as religion, in Ralph Erskine.'

❦ ❦ ❦

A HYMN OF TRUST

Genesis 28.20–2

O God of Bethel! By whose hand
Thy people still are fed;
Who through this weary pilgrimage
Hast all our fathers led:

Our vows, our pray'rs, we now present
Before thy throne of grace:
God of our fathers! Be the God
Of their succeeding race.

Through each perplexing path of life
Our wand'ring footsteps guide;
Give us each day our daily bread,
And raiment fit provide.

O spread thy cov'ring wings around,
Till all our wand'rings cease,
And at our Father's loved abode
Our souls arrive in peace.

Such blessings from thy gracious hand
Our humble prayers implore;
And thou shalt be our chosen God,
And portion evermore.

Scottish Paraphrases (1781), no. 2.

While metrical versions of the Old Testament Psalms were an essential component of worship in Scotland from the 1560s onward, hymns based on other Scriptural passages had to wait, interestingly enough, until the century of Enlightenment. In 1742, the General Assembly appointed a committee to produce 'scriptural songs' in translation, and three years later *45 Translations and Paraphrases*, from both Old Testament and New Testament, made its appearance. But the times were not propitious (it was the year of the great Jacobite rising), and a generation elapsed before another committee was set up to revise and expand the earlier work. The result appeared in 1781 as *Translations and Paraphrases in Verse of several passages in Sacred Scripture*. Never formally authorised by the General Assembly, the Paraphrases (often printed at the end of the Bible, after the Metrical Psalter) eventually established themselves as a treasured element in congregational praise and family devotions. The committee responsible for the 1781 volume included such distinguished churchmen as Hugh Blair of St Giles' and Alexander Carlyle of Inveresk; but they drew upon the existing work of several able writers: English Independents like Isaac Watts and Philip Doddridge, and Church of Scotland ministers like John Morison of Canisbay, William Cameron (eventually of Kirknewton: a genius at revision), and John Logan of South Leith (though there is still dispute as to whether what he claimed as his own was really attributable to Michael Bruce).

The best of the Paraphrases are remarkable both for their faithfulness to the Biblical text and their felicity of expression; and supreme among them is the Second, which – though based on a hymn by Philip Doddridge entitled 'Jacob's Vow' – was extensively revised by John Logan and others for the 1781 edition. As James Moffatt remarked in his *Handbook to the Church Hymnary* (1927), 'It rarely happens that such a strangely composite production should result in a hymn of such great excellence which holds a place in the affections of all Scotsmen second only to "The Lord's my Shepherd, I'll not want".'

❦ ❦ ❦

A HYMN OF PENITENCE AND CONFIDENCE

Hosea 6.1–4

Come, let us to the Lord our God
With contrite hearts return;
Our God is gracious, nor will leave
The desolate to mourn.

His voice commands the tempest forth,
And stills the stormy wave;
And though his arm be strong to smite,
'Tis also strong to save.

Long hath the night of sorrow reigned,
The dawn shall bring us light;
God shall appear, and we shall rise
With gladness in his sight.

Our hearts, if God we seek to know,
Shall know him, and rejoice;
His coming like the morn shall be,
Like morning songs his voice.

As dew upon the tender herb,
Diffusing fragrance round;
As showers that usher in the spring,
And cheer the thirsty ground:

So shall his presence bless our souls,
And shed a joyful light;
That hallowed morn shall chase away
The sorrows of the night.

Scottish Paraphrases (1781), no. 30.

John Morison (1750–98), the author of this remarkable hymn (none the worse for its relatively slight connection with the prophet Hosea's words), was an Aberdonian who spent most of his life in Caithness, first as a school-teacher and then as a minister. Introduced to the Assembly Committee at work on the Paraphrases by the egregious John Logan, then tutoring the young Sir John Sinclair of Ulbster, he submitted a number of pieces, seven of which were accepted. These included Paraphrase 19, 'The race that long in darkness pined', and Paraphrase 35, ''Twas on that night' (a version of Matthew 26.26–9 on the institution of the Lord's Supper). Morison was ordained to the parish of Canisbay in 1780. Appointed to membership of the Paraphrases Committee, he also wrote the account of Canisbay for Sinclair's first *Statistical Account*, and the topographical history of Caithness for Chalmers' *Caledonia*. His career is a reminder of the contribution made to Scottish culture by workers in what – to some of Edinburgh's *literati* – may have seemed remote or even outlandish parts of the country.

❧ ❧ ❧
A HYMN OF TRUST IN THE SAVIOUR
Romans 8.33–9

The Saviour dy'd, but rose again
Triumphant from the grave;
And pleads our cause at God's right hand,
Omnipotent to save.

Who then can e'er divide us more
From Jesus and his love,
Or break the sacred chain that binds
The earth to heaven above?

Let troubles rise, and terrors frown,
And days of darkness fall;
Through him all dangers we'll defy,
And more than conquer all.

Nor death nor life, nor earth nor hell,
Nor time's destroying sway,
Can e'er efface us from his heart,
Or make his love decay.

Each future period that will bless,
As it has blessed the past;
He lov'd us from the first of time,
He loves us to the last.

Scottish Paraphrases (1781), no. 48, verses 5–9.

Though subsequently revised in committee, this great paraphrase of one of the sublimest passages in all Scripture first came – paradoxically enough – from the pen of the more than slightly disreputable John Logan. An associate of some of the leading figures in the Edinburgh Enlightenment, Logan was ordained to the second charge of the parish of South Leith in 1773, and appointed a member of the Paraphrases Committee two years later. Most of the committee's work seems to have been left to Logan and the youthful William Cameron, and their achievements were outstanding. For various reasons, Logan's reputation fell under a cloud. He resigned his charge, spending the last years of his life in London; and controversy still continues as to whether certain poems whose authorship he claimed were written by him or his one-time fellow student, Michael Bruce.

❄ ❄ ❄

A HYMN OF DEDICATION

2 Timothy 1.11–12

I'm not ashamed to own my Lord,
Or to defend his cause,
Maintain the glory of his cross,
And honour all his laws.

Jesus, my Lord! I know his name,
His name is all my boast;
Nor will he put my soul to shame,
Nor let my hope be lost.

I know that safe with him remains,
Protected by his pow'r,
What I've committed to his trust,
Till the decisive hour.

Then will he own his servant's name
Before his Father's face,
And in the New Jerusalem
Appoint my soul a place.

Scottish Paraphrases (1781), no. 54.

Isaac Watts (1674–1748), to whom we owe the original version of this paraphrase, wrote several hundred hymns, and is generally regarded, with Charles Wesley, as one of the greatest of English hymn-writers. Four of the Paraphrases originated with him: number 54 ('I'm not ashamed to own my Lord'), number 61 ('Blest be the everlasting God'), number 63 ('Behold the amazing gift of love'), and number 66 ('How bright these glorious spirits shine'). An English Independent (Congregationalist), Watts was for a short time pastor of an important congregation in London; but his health failed, and he spent the remainder of his days as the guest of Sir Thomas and Lady Abney at their luxurious homes in the neighbourhood of the capital. Author of a great variety of works, philosophical and literary, he owes his lasting fame to such hymns as 'Jesus shall reign where'er the sun', 'When I survey the wondrous cross', 'Come let us join our cheerful songs', and 'Our God, our help in ages past' – all characterised, it has been said, by 'tender faith, joyousness, and serene piety'. When Edinburgh University conferred the DD degree upon him, Samuel Johnson remarked: 'Academic honours would have more value if they were always bestowed with equal judgment'.

William Cameron (1751–1811), who revised Watts' work for the 1781 edition of the *Paraphrases*, and had a hand in many other revisions, became minister of Kirknewton, near Edinburgh, in 1786. He was the author of a number of publications, including two or three volumes of poetry.

When on his death-bed, the celebrated Victorian evangelist, Henry Drummond, had Paraphrase 54 sung to him, and at its conclusion remarked, 'There's nothing to beat that.'

❦ ❦ ❦
FELLOW-SUFFERER AND SAVIOUR

Hebrews 4.14–16

Where high the heav'nly temple stands,
The house of God not made with hands,
A great High Priest our nature wears,
The guardian of mankind appears.

He who for men their surety stood,
And poured on earth his precious blood,
Pursues in heav'n his mighty plan,
The Saviour and the friend of man.

Though now ascended up on high,
He bends on earth a brother's eye;
Partaker of the human name,
He knows the frailty of our frame.

Our fellow-suff'rer yet retains
A fellow-feeling of our pains;
And still remembers in the skies
His tears, his agonies, and cries.

In ev'ry pang that rends the heart,
The Man of sorrows had a part;
He sympathizes with our grief,
And to the suff'rer sends relief.

With boldness, therefore, at the throne,
Let us make all our sorrows known;
And ask the aids of heavenly pow'r
To help us in the evil hour.

Scottish Paraphrases (1781), no. 58.

The original author of this impressive paraphrase may have been Michael Bruce (1746–67), the school-teacher and poet from Kinnesswood, near Kinross, who died of consumption while still young. But John Logan (1748–88) published it as his own in 1781, and it was further altered before appearing in the *Paraphrases* that same year. As James Moffatt wisely observed on the Bruce–Logan controversy in his *Handbook to the Church Hymnary* (1927), 'The fact that instructed opinion is so acutely divided suggests that a final solution is scarcely possible.' Undeterred by this problem, several generations of Scottish worshippers found their faith strengthened by such memorable phrases as 'In ev'ry pang that rends the heart the Man of Sorrows had a part'.

❧ ❧ ❧
THE ENVIRONMENT OF THE FAITHFUL

Hebrews 12.1, 2 and 12

Behold what witnesses unseen
Encompass us around;
Men once like us with suff'ring try'd
But now with glory crown'd.

Let us with zeal like theirs inspired,
Begin the Christian race,
And, freed from each encumbering weight
Their holy footsteps trace.

Behold a witness nobler still,
Who trod affliction's path,
Jesus, at once the finisher
And author of our faith.

He for the joy before him set,
So generous was his love,
Endured the cross, despised the shame,
And now he reigns above . . .

Then let our hearts no more despond,
Our hands be weak no more;
Still let us trust our Father's love,
His wisdom still adore.

Scottish Paraphrases (1781), no. 59.

Scottish Paraphrases (1781) names no author for this meditation on the Communion of Saints and the contrast between the sufferings of earth and the joys of heaven.

An eloquent twentieth-century reflection on the same theme occurs in John Baillie's *Invitation to Pilgrimage* (1942, pp. 115–16), in the chapter entitled, 'Traveller's Joy and Pain':

> When all is said, however, the deepest tragedy of life resides, not in those sufferings which seem to fall in such different measure on different men, but in such conditions of earthly existence as are common to us all. The ultimate sadness is that nothing lasts; that the bloom so soon disappears from all things that are young, that the vigour of maturity is so short-lived, while age brings weariness and forgetfulness and decay such as presage the oblivion and corruption of the grave. This is why 'our sincerest laughter with some pain is fraught'. To call to mind the care-free days of youth, to see the friends of youth disappear one by one from our earthly company with hopes only half fulfilled and work only half done, and to know that no task of our own can ever be completed or any joy held in possession for more than a few fleeting years – that is our great heaviness of heart. And for it I know no healing, nor for the problem of suffering any final prospect of solution, save as we are able to share St. Paul's faith when he cries, 'For I reckon that the sufferings of this present time are not worthy to be compared with the glory which shall be revealed to us'. About our human suffering, therefore, Christianity has ultimately the same thing to say as about our human sin – it repeats to us the story of the life and suffering and death and resurrection of Jesus Christ.

A PRAYER FOR GRACE

Hebrews 13.20, 21

Father of peace and God of love!
We own thy pow'r to save,
That pow'r by which our Shepherd rose
Victorious o'er the grave.

Him from the dead thou brought'st again,
When, by his precious blood,
Confirm'd and seal'd for evermore,
Th'eternal cov'nant stood.

O may thy Spirit seal our souls,
And mould them to thy will,
That our weak hearts no more may stray,
But keep thy precepts still;

That to perfection's sacred height
We nearer still may rise,
And all we think, and all we do,
Be pleasing in thine eyes.

Scottish Paraphrases (1781), no. 60.

A nother composite production – much of it drawing upon the words of Philip Doddridge (1702–51), the English Congregationalist, published in his *Hymns* of 1755, but with verse 4 by William Cameron, the supreme adapter. Doddridge, whose original hymn bore the appropriate title, 'The Christian perfected by the Grace of God in Christ', was one of the most learned and influential of eighteenth-century Dissenters. The greater part of his mature life was spent in charge of a seminary at Northampton which had many of the characteristics of a university. His *The Rise and Progress of Religion in the Soul* gained him an international reputation, and his hymns included 'O God of Bethel', 'Hark the glad sound', and 'Father of peace and God of love'.

❊ ❊ ❊

THE RESURRECTION HOPE

1 Peter 1.3–5

Bless'd be the everlasting God,
The Father of our Lord;
Be his abounding mercy praised,
His majesty adored.

When from the dead he rais'd his Son,
And called him to the sky,
He gave our souls a lively hope
That they should never die.

To an inheritance divine
He taught our hearts to rise;
'Tis uncorrupted, undefiled,
Unfading in the skies.

Saints by the pow'r of God are kept
Till the salvation come;
We walk by faith as strangers here;
But Christ shall call us home.

Scottish Paraphrases (1781), no. 61.

The greater part of this meditation on the Resurrection and Ascension of Christ is the work of Isaac Watts (*Hymns*, 1707), but the ever-reliable William Cameron provided verse 3.

❦ ❦ ❦
THE JOYS OF HEAVEN

Revelation 7.13–17

How bright these glorious spirits shine!
Whence all their white array?
How came they to the seats of everlasting day?
Lo! These are they from sufferings great
Who came to realms of light,
And in the blood of Christ have wash'd
Those robes which shine so bright.

Now, with triumphal palms, they stand
Before the throne on high,
And serve the God they love, amidst
The glories of the sky.
His presence fills each heart with joy,
Tunes ev'ry mouth to sing:
By day, by night, the sacred courts
With glad hosannas ring.

Hunger and thirst are felt no more,
Nor suns with scorching ray;
God is their sun, whose cheering beams
Diffuse eternal day.
The Lamb which dwells amidst the throne
Shall o'er them still preside;
Feed them with nourishment divine,
And all their footsteps guide.

'Mong pastures green he'll lead his flock
Where living streams appear;
And God the Lord from ev'ry eye
shall wipe off ev'ry tear.

Scottish Paraphrases (1781), no. 66.

A gain we are indebted to one of the hymns of Isaac Watts (1674–1748) – revised by William Cameron – for this remarkably faithful versification of a key passage in the Revelation of St John.

Although the eschatological language of the Paraphrase, and its New Testament original, is unfamiliar to modern minds, an early twentieth-century comment by a Scottish theologian, J. H. Leckie, may prove illuminating. Writing that 'the apocalyptic element in our religion is a permanent thing, belonging to its essential genius', he goes on:

> St. John and the other prophets of his kind were no such childish literalists as their censors suppose them to have been. A writer capable of such profound sayings as 'the Lamb slain from the foundation of the world' was quite able to distinguish form from substance, and to perceive the spiritual meanings of his own symbolism. These pictures of St. John signify victory, peace, consolation, worship, knowledge, and the fullness of perfect being. And no modern writer has ever been able to suggest imagery that can take their place . . .The apocalyptic imagery of future blessedness, like the apocalyptic forms of belief, is consecrated by immemorial tradition; it is the fruit of history; and it has a message for the simplest mind as well as for the wise and understanding. It is vivid; it is fraught with plain spiritual meanings; it appeals to tender human emotions; and it is the symbol of a high romance. For all these reasons it has endured, and is likely to endure to the end.
>
> J. H. Leckie, *The World to Come and Final Destiny* (1918), p. 319.

THE COTTER'S SATURDAY NIGHT

The cheerful' supper done, wi' serious face
They, round the ingle, form a circle wide;
The sire turns o'er, wi' patriarchal grace
The big ha' Bible, ance his father's pride
His bonnet reverently is laid aside,
His lyart haffets wearing thin and bare;
Those strains that once did sweet in Zion glide,
He wales a portion with judicious care,
And 'Let us worship God' he says, with solemn air.

They chant their artless notes in simple guise,
They tune their hearts, by far the noblest aim;
Perhaps Dundee's wild-warbling measures rise,
Or plaintive *Martyrs*, worthy of the name;
Or noble *Elgin* beets the heavenward flame,
The sweetest far of Scotia's holy lays:
Compared with these Italian trills are tame;
The tickled ears no heart-felt raptures raise;
Nae unison hae they, with our Creator's praise.

The priest-like father reads the sacred page,
How Abram was the friend of God on high;
Or, Moses bade eternal warfare wage
With Amalek's ungracious progeny;
Or, how the royal Bard did groaning lie
Beneath the stroke of Heaven's avenging ire;
Or Job's pathetic plaint, and wailing cry;
Or rapt Isaiah's wild seraphic fire;
Or other holy Seers that tune the sacred lyre.

Perhaps the Christian volume is the theme:
How guiltless blood for guilty man was shed;
How He, who bore in Heaven the second name,
Had not on earth whereon to lay His head;
How His first followers and servants sped;
The precepts sage they wrote to many a land:
How he, who lone in Patmos banished,

Saw in the son a mighty angel stand,
And heard great Bab'lon's doom pronounced by Heaven's command.

Then kneeling down to Heaven's Eternal King,
The saint, the father, and the husband prays:
Hope 'springs exulting on triumphant wing',
That thus they all shall meet in future days,
There, ever bask in uncreated rays,
No more to sigh or shed the bitter tear,
Together hymning their Creator's praise,
In such society, yet still more dear;
While circling Time moves round in an eternal sphere.

Compared with this, how poor Religion's pride,
In all the pomp of method and of art;
When men display to congregations wide
Devotion's every grace, except the heart
The Power, incens'd, the pageant will desert,
The pompous strain, the sacerdotal stole;
But haply, in some cottage far apart,
May hear, well-pleased, the language of the soul,
And in His Book of Life the inmates poor enrol.

Then homeward all take off their several way;
The youngling cottagers retire to rest:
The parent-pair their secret homage pay,
And proffer up to Heaven the warm request,
That He who stills the raven's clamorous nest,
And decks the lily fair in flow'ry pride,
Would, in the way His wisdom sees the best,
For them and for their little ones provide;
But, chiefly, in their hearts with Grace Divine preside . . .

From Robert Burns, 'The Cotter's Saturday Night' (c.1785).

No one would presume to cite Robert Burns (1759–96) as an exemplary Christian; but his was a very complex character, and the Rabelaisian aspects of it – and his inimitable lampooning of the absurd and repulsive features of high Calvinism as late eighteenth-century Scotland understood or misunderstood it – should not be allowed to obscure his unaffected appreciation of traditional Scottish religion. There may be something a little cloying in his representation of it in 'The Cottar's Saturday Night', but there is sincerity too; and the much-quoted verses, reminiscent no doubt of family devotions in the Ayrshire farmhouse of his youth, cannot be dismissed as lacking foundation in fact.

Nineteenth
Century

❋ ❋ ❋
RELIGION IN ANNANDALE c. 1800

Annandale was not an irreligious country, – though Annan itself (owing to a drunken Clergyman, and the logical habits they cultivated) was more given to sceptical free-thinking than other places; – the greatly prevailing fashion was, a decent form of devoutness, and pious theoretically anxious regard for things Sacred; in all which the Irving Household stood fairly on a level with its neighbours, or perhaps above most of them. They went duly to Kirk; strove still to tolerate and almost to respect their unfortunate Minister (who had succeeded a father greatly esteemed in that office, and was a man of gifts himself, and of much good-nature, though so far gone astray); nothing of profane, I believe, or of the least tendency that way, was usually seen, or would have been suffered without protest and grave rebuke in Irving's environment near or remote. At the same time this other fact was visible enough, if you examined: 'A man who awoke to the belief that he actually had a soul to be saved or lost was apt to be found among the Dissenting people, and to have given up attendance on the Kirk.' It was ungentle for him to attend the Meeting-house; but he found it to be altogether salutary. This was the case, throughout, in Irving's district and mine,– as I had remarked for myself, nobody teaching me, at an early period of my investigations into men and things. I concluded that it would be generally so over Scotland; but found when I went north, to Edinburgh, Glasgow, Fife, etc. that it was not, or by no means so perceptibly was. For the rest, all Dissent in Scotland is merely a stricter adherence to the National Kirk in all points; and the then Dissenterage is definable to moderns simply as a 'Free Kirk making no noise.' It had quietly (about 1740), after much haggle and remonstrance, 'seceded' or walked out of its stipends, official ties and dignities, greatly to the mute sorrow of religious Scotland; and was still, in a strict manner, on the united voluntary principle, preaching to the people what of best and sacredest it could. Not that there was not something of rigour, of severity; a lean-minded controversial spirit among certain brethren (mostly of the laity, I think); 'narrow-nebs' (narrow of neb, i.e. of nose or bill) as the outsiders called them; of flowerage, or free harmonious beauty, there could not well be much in this system: but really, except on stated occasions (annual feast-day, for instance, when you were reminded that 'a testimony had been lifted up', which *you were* now the bearers of), there was little, almost no talk, especially no preaching at all about 'patronage', or secular controversy; but all turned on the weightier and universal matters of the Law, and was considerably entitled to say for itself, 'Hear, all men.' Very venerable are those old Seceder Clergy to me now, when I look back on them. Most of the chief figures among them, in Irving's time and mine, were hoary old men. Men so like what one might call antique 'Evangelists in modern vesture, and Poor Scholars and Gentlemen of Christ', I have nowhere met with in monasteries or Churches, among Protestant or Papal Clergy, in any country of the world.

Thomas Carlyle, *Reminiscences* (Everyman edn, 1932), pp. 176–7.

The sudden death of his wife in 1866 released a flood of memories in Thomas Carlyle (1795–1881), taking him back to the early days of the century, to his parents, to his great friend Edward Irving, and to the religious life of Annandale on the Scottish Borders (whose influence he never escaped). This vivid tribute comes from his essay on Irving.

❄ ❄ ❄
SIR WALTER SCOTT'S PHILOSOPHY

Scott had not the metaphysical turn of his countrymen, and he had no instinct to preach, but the whole of his life and work was based on a reasoned philosophy of conduct. Its cornerstones were humility and discipline. The life of man was difficult, but not desperate, and to live it worthily you must forget yourself and love others. The failures were the egotists who were wrapped up in self, the doctrinaires who were in chains to a dogma, the Pharisees who despised their brethren. In him the 'common sense' of the eighteenth century was coloured and lit by Christian charity. Happiness could only be attained by unselfregarding. He preaches this faith through the mouth of Jeanie Deans – indeed it is the basis of all his ethical portraiture, it crops up everywhere in his letters and *Journal*, and in his review of Canto III of *Childe Harold* in the *Quarterly* he expounds it to Byron and labours to reconcile him with the world. This paper should not be forgotten, for in it Scott professes explicitly his moral code. Its axiom is that there is no royal road to heart's ease, but that there is a path for the humble pilgrim. The precepts for such are –

> to narrow our wishes and desires within the scope of our present powers of attainment; to consider our misfortunes as our inevitable share in the patrimony of Adam; to bridle those irritable feelings which, ungoverned, are sure to become governors; to shun that intensity of galling and self-wounding reflection which our poet has described in his own burning language; to stoop, in short, to the realities of life, repent if we have offended, and pardon if we have been trespassed against; to look at the world less as our foe than as a doubtful and capricious friend whose applause we ought so far as possible to deserve, but neither to court nor to condemn.

To this philosophy he added a stalwart trust in the Christian doctrines, a trust which was simple, unqualified and unquestioning. His was not a soul to be troubled by doubts or to be kindled to mystical fervour, though he was ready to admit the reality of the latter. There is a passage in the *Journal* where he defends the work of Methodism as 'carrying religion into classes in society where it would scarce be found to penetrate, did it rely merely upon proof of its doctrines, upon calm reasoning and upon rational argument'. But such excitements were not for him; for his mind to seek them would have been like drug-taking, a renunciation of self-discipline. In the Scotland of his day this teaching was much in season. The old fires of Calvinism had burned too murkily, the light of the *Aufklarung* had been too thin and cold, but in Scott was a spirit which could both illumine and comfort his world. He gave it a code of ethics robuster because more rational, and he pointed the road to a humaner faith.

John Buchan, Sir Walter Scott (1932), pp. 369–70.

The reputation of Sir Walter Scott (1772–1832), whether as poet or as novelist, has plummeted more dramatically in the last hundred years or so than almost any other British writer's. He is perhaps due for a revival, but one thing at least is well nigh incontestable: his greatness as a man. This comes out very clearly in the estimate of his philosophy of life, taken from John Buchan's fine biography.

❦ ❦ ❦
THOMAS CHALMERS PREACHES IN TWEEDDALE

We well remember our first hearing Dr. Chalmers. We were in a moorland district in Tweeddale, rejoicing in the country, after nine months of the High School. We heard that a famous preacher was to be at a neighbouring parish church, and off we set, a cartful of irrepressible youngsters. 'Calm was all nature as a resting wheel'. The crows, instead of making wing, were impudent and sat still; the horses were standing, knowing the day, at the field-gates, gossiping and gazing, idle and happy; the moor was stretching away in the pale sunlight – vast, dim, melancholy, like a sea; everywhere were to be seen the gatherings of people, 'sprinklings of blithe company'; the countryside seemed moving to one centre. As we entered the kirk we saw a notorious character, a drover, who had much of the brutal look of what he worked in, with the knowing eye of the man of the city, a sort of big Peter Bell –

He had a hardness in his eye,
He had a hardness in his cheek.

He was our terror, and we not only wondered, but were afraid when we saw him going in. The kirk was full as it could hold. How different in looks to a brisk town congregation! There was a fine leisureliness and vague stare; all the dignity and vacancy of animals; eyebrows raised and mouths open, as is the habit with those who speak little and look much, and at far-off objects. The minister comes in, homely in his dress and gait, but having a great look about him, like a mountain among hills. The High School boys thought him like a 'big one of ourselves', he looks vaguely round his audience, as if he saw in it *one great object, not many*. We shall never forget his smile! Its general benignity; – how he let the light of his countenance fall on us! He read a few verses quietly; then prayed briefly, silently, with his eyes wide open all the time, but not seeing. Then he gave out his text; we forget it, but its subject was, 'Death reigns'. He stated slowly, calmly, the simple meaning of the words; what death was, and how and why it reigned; then suddenly he started, and looked like a man who had seen some great sight, and was breathless to declare it; he told us how death reigned – everywhere, at all times, in all places; how we all knew it, how we would yet know more of it. The drover, who had sat down in the table-seat opposite, was gazing up in a state of stupid excitement; he seemed restless, but never kept his eye from the speaker. The tide set in – everything added to its power, deep called to deep, imagery and illustration poured in; and every now and then the theme – the simple, terrible statement, was repeated in some lucid interval. After overwhelming us with proofs of the reign of Death, and transferring to us his intense energy and emotion; and after shrieking, as if in despair, these words, 'Death is a tremendous necessity', – he suddenly looked beyond us as to some distant region, and cried out, 'Behold a mightier! – who is this? He cometh from Edom, with dyed garments from Bozrah, glorious in his apparel, speaking in righteousness, travelling in the greatness of his strength, mighty to save.'

J. Brown, *Horae Subsecivae* (3-vol. edn, 1908),'2nd Series', pp. 143–6.

Not long after the death of Thomas Chalmers (1780–1847), Dr John Brown wrote a review of the great man's posthumous works which developed into one of the finest biographical studies of the Victorian age. It is full of good things, but one of the most arresting passages is an account of the impression made upon a young hearer (Brown himself) by a sermon which Chalmers had preached in Upper Tweeddale many years before. Those who find the story somewhat exaggerated should perhaps be reminded that the sour and cynical William Hazlitt was driven to quote from *Othello* to describe the preacher's impact: 'There's magic in the web!' – and that Lord Jeffrey, editor of the *Edinburgh Review* (who could be a fierce critic) once remarked, after hearing Chalmers speak in the General Assembly of 1816, 'There is something altogether remarkable about that man. It reminds me more of what one reads of as the effect of the eloquence of Demosthenes than anything I ever heard.'

On Chalmers, the outstanding Scottish minister of the nineteenth century, two works are indispensable: W. Hanna, *Memoirs of Dr Chalmers* (4 vols, 1849–52), and S. J. Brown, *Thomas Chalmers and the Godly Commonwealth in Scotland* (1982).

John Brown (1810–82) was a delightful essayist – comparable in many ways with the great Charles Lamb – who practised medicine in Edinburgh for many years, and whose writings, collected in three volumes under the title *Horae Subsecivae*, included the celebrated 'Rab and his Friends'. Himself a member of the formidable Brown dynasty (his father, John Brown, was minister of Broughton Place Church and professor in the United Presbyterian College in Edinburgh; his grandfather, John Brown of Haddington, author of the once-renowned *Self-Interpreting Bible*), Brown provides us with some of the most vivid and arresting pictures of religious life in late-eighteenth- and early-nineteenth-century Scotland. In the present volume, three entries are from his pen: that on his uncle, Ebenezer Brown (below, p. 84), this description of Chalmers preaching, and the charming portrait of 'Jeems the Doorkeeper' (below, p. 86).

❊ ❊ ❊
THE SABBATH IN GLASGOW, 1819

One of the most remarkable features which I have observed in the manners of the Scottish people, is their wonderfully strict observance of the Sabbath – and this strictness seems to be carried to a still greater height here than even in Edinburgh. The contrast which the streets afford on this day, to every other day in the week, is indeed most striking. They are all as deserted and still during the hours of divine service, as if they belonged to a City of the Dead. Not a sound to be heard from end to end, except perhaps a solitary echo answering here and there to the step of some member of my own profession – the only class of persons who, without some considerable sacrifice of character, may venture to be seen abroad at an hour so sacred. But then what a throng and bustle while the bell is ringing – one would think every house had emptied itself from garret to cellar – such is the endless stream that pours along, gathering as it goes, towards every place from which that all-attractive solemn summons is heard. The attire of the lower orders, on these occasions, is particularly gay and smart; above all of the women, who bedizen themselves in this mercantile city in a most gorgeous manner indeed. They seem almost all to sport silk stockings and clean gloves, and large tufts of feathers float from every bonnet; and every one carries a richly-bound Bible and Psalm-book in her hand, as the most conspicuous part of all her finery, unless when there is a threatening of rain, in which case the same precious books are carried wrapt up carefully in the folds of a snow-white pocket-handkerchief. When the service is over at any particular place of worship – (for which moment the Scotch have, in their language, an appropriate and picturesque term, the *kirk-skailing*,) – the rush is, of course, still more huge and impetuous. To advance up a street in the teeth of one of their congregations coming forth in this way, is as impossible as it would be to skull up a cataract. There is nothing for it but facing about, and allowing yourself to be borne along, submissive and resigned, with the furious and conglomerated roll of this human tide. I never saw anything out of Scotland that bore the least resemblance to this; even the emptying of a London theatre is a joke to the stream that wedges up the whole channel of the main street of Glasgow, when the congregation of one of the popular ministers of the place begins to disperse itself. For the most part, the whole of the pious mass moves in perfect silence; and if you catch a few low words from some group that advances by your side, you are sure to find them the vehicles of nothing but some criticism on what has just been said by the preacher. Altogether, the effect of the thing is prodigious, and would, in one moment, knock down the whole prejudices of the Quarterly Reviewer, or any other English High-Churchman, who thinks the Scotch a nation of sheer infidels.

J. G. Lockhart, *Peter's Letters to his Kinsfolk*
(ed. W. Roddick, 1977), pp. 168–9.

John Gibson Lockhart (1794–1854), one of the leading men of letters of his day, novelist and editor of the *Quarterly Review* from 1825 to 1853, married Sir Walter Scott's daughter Sophia and later published a celebrated biography of the great man.

In *Peter's Letters to his Kinsfolk* Lockhart provided vivid descriptions of various aspects of early nineteenth-century Scottish society, including this – perhaps only slightly exaggerated – picture of church-going and the central place it occupied in national life between Waterloo and the Disruption.

❧ ❧ ❧
EBENEZER BROWN AND THE CARTERS

Uncle Ebenezer, with all his mildness and complaisance, was, like most of the Browns, *tenax propositi*, firm to obstinacy. He had established a week-day sermon at the North Ferry, about two miles from his own town, Inverkeithing. It was, I think on the Tuesdays. It was winter, and a wild, drifting, and dangerous day; and his daughters – his wife was dead – besought him not to go; he smiled vaguely, but continued getting into his big-coat. Nothing would stay him, and away he and the pony stumbled through the dumb and blinding snow. He was half-way on his journey, and had got into the sermon he was going to preach, and was utterly insensible to the outward storm; his pony getting its feet *balled*, staggered about, and at last upset his master and himself into the ditch at the roadside. The feeble, heedless, rapt old man might have perished there, had not some carters, bringing up whisky casks from the Ferry, seen the catastrophe, and rushed up, raising him, and *dichting* him, with much commiseration and blunt speech – 'Puir auld man, what brocht ye here on sic a day?' There they were, a rough crew, surrounding the saintly man, some putting on his hat, sorting and cheering him, others knocking the balls off the pony's feet, and stuffing them with grease. He was most polite and grateful, and one of these cordial ruffians having pierced a cask, brought him a horn of whisky, and said, 'Tak that, it'll hearten ye'. He took the horn, and bowing to them, said, 'Sirs, let us give thanks!' and there, by the roadside, in the drift and storm, he asked a blessing on it, and for his kind deliverers, and took a tasting of the horn. The men cried like children. They lifted him on his pony, one going with him, and when the rest arrived in Inverkeithing, they repeated the story to everybody, and broke down in tears whenever they came to the blessing. 'And to think o' askin a blessing on a tass o'whisky!' Next Presbytery day, after the ordinary business was over, he rose up – he seldom spoke – and said, 'Moderator, I have something personal to myself to say. I have often said, that real kindness belongs only to true Christians, but' – and then he told the story of these men; 'but more true kindness I never experienced than from these lads. They may have had the grace of God, I don't know; but I never mean again to be so *positive* in speaking of this matter.'

J. Brown, 'Letter to John Cairns', Horae Subsecivae
(3-vol. edn, 1908), '2nd Series', pp. 74–5.

A mong the Presbyterian Dissenters of eighteenth and nineteenth-century Scotland none were more highly regarded than the priestly family descended from John Brown (1722–87), generally known as 'John Brown of Haddington': the herd-boy who taught himself Latin, Greek and Hebrew, served as minister of the 'Burgher' Secession church in Haddington for over thirty years, and became famous as the author of the *Self-Interpreting Bible*, a plain commentary which proved immensely popular. John Brown's second son, Ebenezer (1758–1836), ministered in the Burgher church of Inverkeithing for the greater part of his life, and earned a reputation as one of the most impressive preachers and devoted pastors of the day. He seems to have been both devout and lovable, and this extract from the pen of his grand-nephew, John Brown the Victorian essayist, suggests that there may have been some truth in the admiring assertion that 'He was held in such veneration that even the children would advance near to the middle of the road and take their caps off to him as he passed.' Perhaps it should also be noted that, as an adherent of the Burgher (as opposed to the Anti-Burgher) Seceders, he was probably more liberal and less belligerent than they – traits which conceivably surface in his recorded remarks to the local presbytery.

JEEMS THE DOORKEEPER

When my father was in Broughton Place Church, we had a doorkeeper called *Jeems*, and a formidable little man and doorkeeper he was; of unknown age and name, for he existed to us, and indeed still exists to me – though he has been in his grave these sixteen years – as *Jeems*, absolute and *per se*, no more needing a surname than did or do Abraham or Isaac, Samson or Nebuchadnezzar.

He dwelt at the head of Big Lochend's Close in the Canongate, at the top of a long stair – ninety-six steps, as I well know – where he had dwelt, all by himself, for five-and-thirty years, and where, in the midst of all sorts of flittings and changes, not a day opened or closed without the well-known sound of *Jeems* at his prayers – his 'exercise' – at 'the Books'. His clear, fearless, honest voice in psalm and chapter, and strong prayer, came sounding through that wide '*land*', like that of one crying in the wilderness.

. . . He was not communicative about his early life. He would some-times speak to me about '*her*', as if I knew who and where she was, and always with a gentleness and solemnity unlike his usual gruff ways. I found out that he had been married when young, and that 'she' (he never named her) and their child died on the same day – the day of its birth. The only indication of married life in his room, was an old and strong cradle, which he had cut down to rock no more, and which he made the depository of his books – a queer collection.

I have said that he had, with a grave smile, *family* worship, morning and evening, never failing. He not only sang his psalm, but gave out or chanted the line in great style; and on seeing me one morning surprised at this, he said, 'Ye see, John, *oo*', meaning himself and his wife, 'began that way.' He had a firm, true voice, and a genuine though roughish gift of singing, and being methodical in all things, he did what I never heard of in anyone else, – he had seven fixed tunes, one of which he sang on its own set day. Sabbath morning it was *French*, which he went through with great *birr*. Monday, *Scarborough*, which he said was like my father cantering. Tuesday, *Coleshill*, that soft, exquisite air – monotonous and melancholy, soothing and vague, like the sea. This day, Tuesday, was the day of the week on which his wife and child died, and he always sang more verses then than on any other. Wednesday was *Irish*; Thursday, *Old Hundred*; Friday, *Bangor*; and Saturday, *Blackburn*, that humdrummest of tunes, 'as long, and lank, and lean, as is the ribbed sea-sand'. He could not defend it, but had some secret reason for sticking to it. As to the evenings, they were just the same tunes in reversed order, only that on Tuesday night he sang *Coleshill* again, thus dropping *Blackburn* for evening work. The children could tell the day of the week by *Jeems's* tune, and would have been as much astonished at hearing *Bangor* on Monday as at finding St. Giles' halfway down the Canongate.

I frequently breakfasted with him. He made capital porridge, and I could get such buttermilk, or at least have such a relish for it, as in those days. *Jeems* is away – gone over to the majority; and I hope I may never forget to be grateful to the dear and queer old man. I think I see and hear him saying his grace over our bickers (porridge bowls), then taking his two books out of the cradle and reading, not without a certain homely majesty, the first verse of the 99th Psalm,

> Th'eternal Lord doth reign as king,
> Let all the people quake;
> He sits between the cherubims,
> Let th'earth be moved and shake;

then launching out into the noble depths of *Irish*. His chapters were long, and his prayers short, very scriptural, but by no means stereotyped, and wonderfully real, *immediate*, as if he was near Him whom he addressed. Anyone hearing the sound and not the words, would say, 'That man is speaking to someone who is with him – who is present', – as he often said to me, 'There's nae gude dune, John, til ye get to *close grups*.'

J. Brown, 'Jeems the Doorkeeper', *Horae Subsecivae*
(3-vol. edn, 1908), pp. 281–8.

John Brown's touching account of 'Jeems the Doorkeeper' is perhaps particularly welcome as giving us a glimpse of *lay* piety. It comes from one of the essays bound up together in *Horae Subsecivae*, and supplements what Brown had to say elsewhere about the life of that remarkable congregation, Broughton Place Church in Edinburgh, during the ministry there of his father.

❦ ❦ ❦

HYMN ON THE REIGN OF CHRIST

Blessing and honour and glory and power,
Wisdom and riches and strength evermore,
Give ye to him who our battle hath won,
Whose are the kingdom, the crown, and the throne.

Into the heaven of the heavens hath he gone;
Sitteth he now in the joy of the throne;
Weareth he now of the kingdom the crown
Singeth he now the new song with his own.

Soundeth the heaven of the heavens with his Name;
Ringeth the earth with his glory and fame;
Ocean and mountain, stream, forest and flower
Echo his praises and tell of his power.

Ever ascendeth the song and the joy;
Ever descendeth the love from on high;
Blessing and honour and glory and praise, –
This is the theme of the songs that we raise.

Give we the glory and praise to the Lamb;
Take we the robe and the harp and the palm;
Sing we the song of the Lamb that was slain,
Dying in weakness but rising to reign.

Horatius Bonar in *The Church Hymnary* (3rd edn, 1973), no. 299.

The three long-lived Bonar brothers, John James (1803–91), Horatius (1808–89), and Andrew Alexander (1810–92), first came to notice in the Church of Scotland in the decades immediately before the Disruption of 1843; and they played an influential part in the Free Church thereafter.

The eldest, John James, spent his entire ministry in Greenock, but the others soon attained national prominence.

The youngest, Andrew Alexander, made his name early as a member of the little group of Evangelical ministers who travelled to Palestine in 1839 and subsequently inspired the inauguration of Christian missions to the Jews. His *Memoir and Remains of R. M. M'Cheyne* (1844) quickly established itself as a treasured volume in many Scottish homes, doing much to promote the distinctive piety – emotional, demonstrative and Puritanical – of the 'school of saints' who had gathered round Dundee's most celebrated preacher and pastor before his premature death. Andrew published many other works, including (significantly) the *Letters of Samuel Rutherford*; and his own posthumous *Diary and Letters* was much acclaimed. He became Moderator of the General Assembly of the Free Church in 1878.

But it was Horatius (Moderator only five years after his brother) who did most to fashion the ideas and attitudes of devout Scots during the Victorian age. His ministries in Kelso and, later, in Edinburgh were hailed as models of dedication and effectiveness. Eschewing all comment on social and political issues and focusing on the cultivation of personal piety; fervently supportive of the revivalism which stirred Scotland in 1840-41 and again (under Moody and Sankey) in the 1870s and 1880s; tirelessly expounding his premillennialist views and staunchly opposing the Biblical criticism of men like Robertson Smith: he wielded his greatest influence through the hymns which poured from his pen. Of them, the judicious James Moffatt wrote that 'The best of them rank with the classics; one or two have been claimed by exacting judges to be the best hymns ever written'. Though some have little appeal to the present generation, others – like 'Glory be to God the Father', 'Here, O my Lord, I see Thee face to face', and 'Light of the world for ever ever shining' – are still much used around the world. 'Blessing and honour and glory and power', which lacks the sugary or lugubrious or overstrained notes sometimes heard from him, is splendidly objective and doxological.

❦ ❦ ❦
IDEALS OF A PIONEER MISSIONARY:
ALEXANDER DUFF

Whenever we make an appeal on behalf of the heathen, it is constantly urged that there are enough of heathen at home – that there is enough of work to be done at home, and why roam for more in distant lands? I strongly suspect that those who are most clamorous in advancing this plea are just the very men who do little, and care less, either for heathen at home or for heathen at a distance. At all events, it is a plea far more worthy of a heathen than of a Christian. It was not thus that the Apostles argued. If it were, they never would have crossed the walls of Jerusalem. There they would have remained contending with unbelieving Jews, till caught by the flames that reduced to ashes the city of their fathers. And if we act on such a plea we may be charged with despising the example of the Apostles, and found loitering at home till overtaken by the flames of the final conflagration. But shall it be brooked, that those who in this Assembly have so far succeeded to their office, should act so contrary a part? Let us pronounce this impossible. I for one can see no contrariety between home and foreign labour . . .

'The field is the world'. And the more we are like God – the more we reflect His image, the more our nature is assimilated to the Divine – the more nearly will we view the world as God has done. 'True friendship', it has been said, 'has no localities'. and so it is with the love of God in Christ. The sacrifice on Calvary was designed to embrace the globe in its amplitude. Let us view the subject as God views it – let us view it as denizens of the universe – and we shall not be bounded in our efforts of philanthropy, short of the north or south pole. Wherever there is a human being, there must our sympathies extend . . .

From a speech in the General Assembly of 1835, in W. Paton,
Alexander Duff: Pioneer of Missionary Education (1923), pp. 108–9.

Notwithstanding the charges of religious bigotry that have been so profusely heaped upon it, this house, like its noble reforming ancestry, has been, is now, and, I trust ever will be, the consistent, the enlightened advocate of all really useful knowledge throughout the wide domain of families, schools and colleges, whether in this or in other lands. And, notwithstanding the charges of secular convergency that have been as abundantly levelled at it, this house, like its noble reforming ancestry, has been, is now, and, I trust, ever will be, the intrepid, the unbending advocate of a thorough Bible instruction, as an essential ingredient in all sound education, whether on the banks of the Forth or on the banks of the Ganges . . .

Let it, then, ever be our distinguishing glory to arbitrate between the advocates of untenable extremes. Let us, on the one hand, disown the bigotry of an unwise pietism, by resolving to patronise to the utmost, as in times past, the cause of sound literature and science – lest, by our negligence, we help to revive the fatal dogma of the dark ages, that what is philosophically true may yet be allowed to be theologically false. And let us, on the other hand, denounce the bigotry of infidelity, or religious indifference, by resolving to uphold the paramount importance of the sacred oracles, in the great work of Christianising and civilising a guilty world. Let us thus hail true literature and true science as our very best auxiliaries – whether in Scotland, or in India, or in any other quarter of the habitable globe. But, in receiving these as friendly allies into our sacred territory, let us resolutely determine that they shall never, never be allowed to usurp the throne, and wield a tyrant's sceptre over it . . .

From a speech in the General Assembly of 1835, in G. Smith,
The Life of Alexander Duff (1900), pp. 162–3.

Few nineteenth-century Scots wielded a more profound and far-reaching influence than Alexander Duff (1806–78). A disciple of Thomas Chalmers, an enthusiastic Evangelical, and the Church of Scotland's first officially-recognised overseas missionary, he arrived in Calcutta (after two shipwrecks!) in 1830, and did not finally return to his native country until 1864. During the intervening years he made himself the leading apologist and spokesman of the missionary enterprise, as in his address to the General Assembly of 1835. At the same time, he campaigned tirelessly and effectively for the view that if India was to be Christianised it would be by the education of its future leaders in Western and Biblical knowledge through the medium of the English language.

His achievements were many and various. He established the largest and most successful Christian school (later, Duff College) in India. He was closely associated with the development of the entire sub-continent's university system. Acting along with T. B. Macaulay and other 'Anglicists', and in contention with the opposing 'Orientalists', he ensured that government-sponsored higher education in India would be in English, not the vernacular.

He poured out a stream of published works in commendation of his missionary ideals. He founded and, for a time, edited the influential *Calcutta Review*. On his retirement from India he became Professor of Missions at the Free Church's New College in Edinburgh. Despite his lamentable prolixity as a public speaker, he was probably the most effective propagandist for Christian missions seen in Scotland before Livingstone; and his basic principles were adopted by the great majority of thinking Christians in his homeland.

✻ ✻ ✻
COMFORT IN PAIN AND SORROW

Be still, my soul: the Lord is on thy side;
Bear patiently the cross of grief or pain;
Leave to thy God to order and provide;
In every change he faithful will remain.
Be still, my soul: thy best, thy heavenly Friend
Through thorny ways leads to a joyful end.

Be still, my soul: thy God doth undertake
To guide the future as he has the past.
Thy hope, thy confidence let nothing shake;
All now mysterious shall be bright at last.
Be still, my soul: the waves and winds still know
His voice who ruled them while he dwelt below.

Be still, my soul: when dearest friends depart,
And all is darkened in the vale of tears,
Then shalt thou better know his love, his heart,
Who comes to soothe thy sorrow and thy fears.
Be still my soul, thy Jesus can repay,
From his own fullness, all he takes away.

Be still, my soul: the hour is hastening on
When we shall be forever with the Lord,
When disappointment, grief, and fear are gone,
Sorrow forgot, love's purest joys restored.
Be still, my soul: when change and tears are past,
All safe and bless'd we shall meet at last.

Katharina von Schlegel (1697–?), trans. Jane Laurie Borthwick
(1813–97), in *The Church Hymnary* (3rd edn, 1973), no. 673.

Jane Borthwick (1813–97) and her sister Mrs Sarah Findlater, the daughters of an Edinburgh banker, collaborated in numerous translations from the German, including *Hymns from the Land of Luther* (four series, 1854–62). Perhaps the most widely used in worship has been Miss Borthwick's 'Be still, my soul', which appeared in *The Scottish Hymnal* (1870) and then in all three of its successors, *The Church Hymnary* (1898), *The Revised Church Hymnary* (1927) and *The Church Hymnary*, 3rd edn (1973). An eloquent expression of trust in the midst of grief, it is most often sung to the tune of Finlandia, adapted from Sibelius's symphonic poem of that name.

STANLEY ON LIVINGSTONE

His religion is not of the theoretical kind, but it is a constant, earnest, sincere practice. It is neither demonstrative nor loud, but manifests itself in a quiet, practical way, and is always at work. It is not aggressive, which sometimes is troublesome if not impertinent. In him religion exhibits its loveliest features; it governs his conduct not only towards his servants but towards the natives, the bigoted Mohammedans, and all who come in contact with him. Without it, Livingstone, with his ardent temperament, his enthusiasm, his high spirit and courage, must have become uncompanionably, and a hard master. Religion has tamed him, and made him a Christian gentleman; the crude and wilful have been refined and subdued; religion has made him the most companionable of men and indulgent of masters – a man whose society is pleasurable to a degree.

From being thwarted and hated in every possible way by the Arabs and half-castes upon his first arrival at Ujiji, he has, through his uniform kindness and mild, pleasant temper, won all hearts. I observed that universal respect was paid to him. Even the Mohammedans never passed his house without calling to pay their compliments, and to say, 'The blessing of God rest on you!' Each Sunday morning he gathers his little flock around him, and reads prayers and a chapter from the Bible, in a natural, unaffected and sincere tone, and afterwards delivers a short address in the Kisawahili language, about the subject read to them, which is listened to with evident interest and attention.

W. G. Blaikie, *Personal Life of David Livingstone* (1880/1917), p. 357.

In October 1871 there took place the celebrated meeting in Central Africa between David Livingstone (1813–73), the Scottish missionary-explorer, and Henry Morton Stanley (1841–1904), the Scots-born journalist then in the employ of the *New York Herald*. Each told his own story of that encounter.

Livingstone wrote:

> When my spirits were at their lowest ebb the good Samaritan was close at hand, for one morning Susi came running at the top of his speed and gasped out, 'An Englishman! I see him' and off he darted to meet him. The American flag at the head of a caravan told of the nationality of the stranger. Bales of goods, baths of tin, huge kettles, cooking pots, tents etc., made me think, 'This must be a luxurious traveller and not one at his wit's end like me'. It was Henry Morton Stanley, the travelling correspondent of the *New York Herald*, sent by James Gordon Bennett, junior, at an expense of more than £4000, to obtain accurate information about Dr Livingstone if living, and if dead to bring home my bones.

Stanley's account is better known:

> I pushed back the crowds, and, passing from the rear, walked down a living avenue of people, until I came in front of the semi-circle of Arabs, in front of which stood the white man with the grey beard. As I advanced slowly towards him I noticed he was pale, looked wearied, and had a grey beard, wore a bluish cap with a faded gold band round it, had on a red-sleeved waistcoat, and a pair of grey tweed trousers. I would have run to him, only I was a coward in the presence of such a mob – would have embraced him, only, he being an Englishman, I did not know how he would receive me; so I did what cowardice and false pride suggested was the best thing – walked deliberately to him, took off my hat, and said: 'Dr. Livingstone, I presume?' 'Yes', said he with a kind smile, lifting his cap slightly. I replace my hat on my head, and he puts on his cap, and we both grasp hands, And then I say aloud: 'I thank God, Doctor, I have been permitted to see you.' He answered, 'I feel thankful that I am here to welcome you.'

A. C. Ross, *David Livingstone; Mission and Empire* (2002), p. 223.

In the light of his later exploits, we may incline to consider Stanley something of a rascal; but the two men seem to have struck up a genuine friendship, and Stanley's tribute to the sick and aged Livingstone has the ring of sincerity about it, painting as it does a charming picture of the man whom 'religion has tamed . . . and made . . . a Christian gentleman.'

❦ ❦ ❦
THE BIBLE: A SCHOLAR'S FAITH

(After quoting various Confessional documents on the
divine inspiration of Scripture, the writer continues as follows:)

This unanimous doctrine of the Reformed Churches is so constructed as
to make the authority of the Bible altogether independent of questions
that may be raised as to the human agencies by which the book came
into its present form. According to the Confessional doctrine it is not a
matter of faith, when the books that record God's Word were written, or
by whom they were written, or how often they were re-edited, changed,
or added to, before the record of revelation was finally completed, or in
what literary form they were cast, or what modes of literary handling
they display, or what their literary merits and demerits may be judged
to be. It is not even asserted by the Confessions that the persons who
gathered and arranged the material of the Bible were under a special
influence of God's Spirit, but only that under God's singular care, lest an
age of His Church should be left without a full and unmistakeable dec-
laration of His saving will, the record of His revealed Word has been so
framed and preserved, that He still speaks in it as clearly as He speaks
by the Apostles and Prophets, and that we, by the witness of the Spirit,
still recognise it as a word breathed forth by God Himself.

If I am asked why I receive Scripture as the Word of God, and as the
only perfect rule of faith and life, I answer with all the fathers of the
Protestant Church, 'Because the Bible is the only record of the redeeming love of God, because in the Bible alone I find God drawing near to
man in Christ Jesus, and declaring to us, in Him, His will for our salvation. And this record I know to be true by the witness of His Spirit in my
heart, whereby I am assured that none other than God Himself is able
to speak such words to my soul.

William Robertson Smith, 'Answer to the Form of Libel now before
the Free Church Presbytery of Aberdeen' (Edinburgh, 1878).

William Robertson Smith (1846–94) was almost certainly the greatest
scholar produced by any of the Scottish Churches in the nineteenth century. Born in the Free Church manse of Keig, Aberdeenshire, he
was educated in Aberdeen, Edinburgh (where he was deeply influenced by

New College's A. B. Davidson), Bonn and Gottingen. Appointed to a professorship in the Aberdeen Free Church College in 1875, he soon aroused a storm of controversy by his critical approach to the Old Testament, first publicised in articles for the *Encyclopaedia Britannica* (9th edn). Two trials followed before the Free Church General Assembly for his alleged undermining of belief in the divine inspiration of Holy Scripture, and in 1881 he was removed from his Chair. The rest of his life was mainly spent in Cambridge, where he became a Fellow of Christ's College and successively University Librarian and Professor of Arabic.

Within twenty years of Smith's deposition from the Aberdeen Chair virtually all the teachers in the Free Church Colleges of Scotland held views similar to his – which, as this extract perhaps makes clear, may have been revolutionary but were not destructive of Christian belief in the Bible as uniquely the Word of God.

❦ ❦ ❦
PARADOXES OF DISCIPLESHIP

Make me a captive, Lord,
And then I shall be free;
Force me to render up my sword,
And I shall conqueror be.
I sink in life's alarms
When by myself I stand;
Imprison me within thine arms,
And strong shall be my hand.

My heart is weak and poor
Until it master find;
It has no spring of action sure –
It varies with the wind.
It cannot freely move
Till thou hast wrought its chain;
Enslave it with thy matchless love,
And deathless it shall reign.

My power is faint and low
Till I have learned to serve;
It wants the needed fire to glow,
It wants the breeze to nerve;
It cannot drive the world,
Until itself be driven;
Its flag can only be unfurled
When thou shalt breathe from heaven.

My will is not my own
Till thou hast made it thine;
If it would reach a monarch's throne
It must its crown resign;
It only stands unbent,
Amid the clashing strife,
When on thy bosom it has leant
And found in thee its life.

George Matheson in *The Church Hymnary* (3rd edn, 1973), no. 445.

Next to Horatius Bonar, George Matheson (1842–1906) was probably the best-known and most honoured Scottish hymn-writer of the nineteenth century. Born in Glasgow, he was educated at the Academy and the University there. After a distinguished career in Arts and Divinity, he entered the ministry of the Church of Scotland and served the parishes of Innellan (1868–86) and St Bernard's, Edinburgh (1886–99). Though almost blind from an early age, he became a celebrated preacher and poured out a steady stream of books and articles, devotional and theological, all of them from a 'Broad Church' standpoint. But it was through his hymns that he wielded the greatest influence.

❈ ❈ ❈
NEW LIFE THROUGH SELF-SURRENDER

O Love that wilt not let me go,
I rest my weary soul in thee:
I give thee back the life I owe,
That in thine ocean depths its flow
May richer, fuller be.

O Light that followest all my way,
I yield my flickering torch to thee;
My heart restores its borrowed ray,
That in thy sunshine's blaze its day
May brighter, fairer be.

O Joy that seekest me through pain,
I cannot close my heart to thee;
I trace the rainbow through the rain,
And feel the promise is not vain,
That morn shall tearless be.

O Cross that liftest up my head,
I dare not ask to fly from thee:
I lay in dust life's glory dead,
And from the ground there blossoms red
Life that shall endless be.

George Matheson, in *The Church Hymnary* (3rd edn, 1973), no. 677.

O Love that wilt not let me go' may not be George Matheson's finest hymn, but it achieved world-wide popularity. His own account of it is interesting, but not entirely reliable:

> My hymn was composed in the manse of Innellan on the evening of 6th June, 1882. [This dating is wrong, the verses having been published in *Life and Work*, the Kirk's own periodical, in January 1882.] . . . Something had happened to me which was known only to myself, and which caused me severe mental suffering. The hymn was the fruit of that suffering. It was the quickest bit of

work I ever did in my life. I had the impression rather of having it dictated to me by some inward voice than of working it out myself. I am quite sure that the whole work was completed in five minutes, and equally sure that it never received at my hands any retouching or correction.

❀ ❀ ❀
A COUNTRY MINISTER'S SPONTANEOUS WORSHIP

He [James McFarlan] had a beautiful tenor voice, and was at times one of the most pleasing singers I ever listened to; but his voice also, like the rest of him, was a thing for the few, – it could not quicken the beating of the heart of the multitude. Nature had made him all through of a fine fibre, and in everything he did, or tried to do, the fineness was visible. My wife tells me of an incident in connection with his singing that may perhaps be mentioned. We had been at Ruthwell, and on a fine summer morning he and she strolled away to have a look at the Cross, which had been newly roofed in. Having examined it they sat down in silence, which continued for two or three minutes: no word between them. Then, without saying anything, he went into the pulpit, where he broke into the fine hymn, 'Art thou weary, art thou languid' as a bird on the bough might break into its song. Having sung it beautifully and without pause to the end, he came down from the pulpit, and they walked out of the church silently, without word of reference to what had been done. They that knew Mr. McFarlan will see reflected here some of the noteworthy traits of his character, and will understand why I have mentioned the incident.

Helen McFarlan, *James McFarlan (minister of Ruthwell, 1870–89)*
(Edinburgh, privately printed, 1892), pp. 107–8: recollections by
the Revd. Thomas Bain, minister of Hutton and Corrie.

*** *** ***
from
LAMENT FOR A DEAD CHILD

'Christian' we named him, eight short years ago,
In part for one we love on earth, in part
For highest ends, – that he might be Christ's own,
Christ's here with us in time, and Christ's in Heaven.
Nor were we wrong in choice of this dear name;
No memory it holds has he defamed:
No light of hope it sheds into the haze
Of dim futurity, but burns more clear
While we remember him and all he was,
Or dream of what he is through Christ's deep love.
But now his sweet flowers wither on his grave,
And all that might have been is naught, like them;
Nor shall we watch his blooming ever more.
Tonight the moonbeams sleep upon the sod;
The mellow August moonbeams, dewy soft,
And red Arcturus crowns the tender west.
Dear Spirit, where art thou? My Boy, my Pride;
Dropt seed-like in the soil, as thine own flowers?
O feeble emblem of thy life to be!
Thou art not dead, though withered be thy form,
And blanched the roses on thy darling cheek;
And stilled thine earnest loving heart for aye.
He is not dead, dear Lord, but lives in Thee:
We know it is so, and our hearts grow calm.
But O, great Father in the heavens, reveal
Thy meaning in this death, nor let us doubt
That though no summer will bring back his bloom,
He lives in all that's fair, – in all our good.
In no sad fading memory alone,
In no pained thought of his last sufferings,
In no poor grief of ours, or wild regret
He lives, but in the light and life of Christ.
In *these* thou art, dear child. Yet where and how
Shall we hereafter meet?

This then is *Death*.
And what is life? To wait and work and pray,
With naught of thee beside me but thy grave?
O more than this, – to work with truer heart,
And freer hand, and deeper trust in God,
Keeping thy Spirit with me through the years:
To pray, till Heaven, thy home, seems near to me,
And prayer grows one long sweet fellowship
With Christ, thy Lord and mine: so wait till God's
Last message comes that I may live with thee.

James McFarlan, in Helen McFarlan, *James McFarlan* (1892), pp. 118–19.

James McFarlan (1845–89) ministered in the quiet Dumfries-shire parish of Ruthwell from 1874 until his death. He attained no prominence in either ecclesiastical or national life; but the memoir by his wife, which appeared in 1892, and the *Selections from Letters and Journals of Ruthwell Manse Life, 1871–1889*, published in 1914, reveal a man of singular gifts and quite considerable charm. By no means a typical orthodox Calvinist (he seems to have been an admirer of such liberal theologians within the sister Establishment south of the Border as F. D. Maurice and William Robertson of Brighton), he also had affinities with the youthful Scoto-Catholic movement; but the only achievement which came near to bringing him celebrity was the removal, at his instigation, of the eighth-century Ruthwell Cross from its place in the grounds of the manse to a new, specially created, site within the parish kirk. He was, however, a highly-regarded pastor, an able preacher (some of whose sermons survive in Helen McFarlan's memoir), and a sensitively poetic observer of nature and humankind. The two extracts given here (one, a picture of the unstudied piety which characterised his life, the other, a bitter-sweet revelation of the intermingled sorrow and faith with which he faced the tragic death of his young son, Christian) are a tribute to one of those who – in George Eliot's phrase – 'lived faithfully a hidden life, and rest in unvisited tombs'.

A LETTER OF CHRISTIAN COMFORT

We have been thinking a great deal about you as well as about Dr. Bruce himself since we heard of the serious nature of his illness. From what the newspapers have said, we are glad to think things have gone well so far, but I suppose anxiety must continue in some degree for some time. Things go on in their slow, relentless way, and that is one of the trials of faith. You cannot doubt that many Christian people are remembering you daily. But the great comfort is that we know our Lord and Master is thinking both of Dr. Bruce and you with those wise, loving, watchful thoughts of His, and that the forces of nature and of disease and of remedies are after all in His hands who causes all things to work together for our good. Even if we believe this, it is not always easy to feel it. But it remains true, and it is an infinite consolation. Who shall separate us from the love of Christ? I often think that to a man of your husband's vigour and energy and extraordinary power of work, the insidious progress of weakening disease must be most trying and depressing. It is of little use for those who are not feeling the strain to try to talk this away. Indeed, what can one say except that we must trust the great Surgeon? I remember my father saying to me late in his life that he could look back on passages of it so painful that at the time it seemed to him intolerable; and yet, looking back, he distinctly saw that these were the passages of his life that were indispensable – he could not have done without them.

But, dear Mrs. Bruce, why should I be running on in topics which he and you know better than I do? For no reason but this – that when Christian was in the Valley, he heard a voice of one rehearsing God's goodness, and it helped him. So when we can do nothing else for one another we can echo to and fro the precious commonplaces of our most wonderful religion. And we can pray.

P. C. Simpson, *The Life of Principal Rainy* (1909), vol. II, pp. 293–4.

Robert Rainy (1826–1906) was, after Thomas Chalmers, the most prominent Scottish churchman of the nineteenth century. In the immediate aftermath of the Ten Years Conflict and the Disruption, he became a minister of the emergent Free Church, serving first in Huntly and then in Edinburgh's prestigious Free High. Called to the Chair of Church History in the New College in 1862, he became Principal there in 1874 and quickly attained a position of dominance in both College and General Assembly. Three times Moderator, he was a dexterous and highly effective clerical statesman. While his opponents (both Free Church conservatives and Church of Scotland defenders of the Establishment) looked on him as 'the unprincipled Principal' or even 'black Rainy', his admirers would have agreed with Gladstone's description of him as 'the greatest living Scotsman'. Though closely associated with the deposition of William Robertson Smith, the Biblical critic, from his Chair in 1881, Rainy moved the Free Church cautiously but firmly in a liberal direction, and presided over the passing, ten years later, of the momentous Declaratory Act which clarified – and amended – its relationship to its 'subordinate standard', the Calvinistic Westminster Confession of Faith. His last great achievement was the Union of the Free and United Presbyterian Churches in 1900 and the United Free Church's weathering of the storm which that Union brought about.

'A Letter of Comfort' was written by Rainy to the wife of one of the most distinguished, and most radical, of Free Church scholars, Professor A. B. Bruce (1831–99) of Glasgow, then in his last illness. It reveals the unswerving faith and sensitively pastoral concern of one whom those who had only a superficial knowledge of him regarded only as an astute and formidable ecclesiastic.

❦ ❦ ❦
A VICTORIAN HERO: HENRY DRUMMOND

In his brief life we saw him pass through two of the greatest trials to which character can be exposed. We watched him, our fellow-student and not yet twenty-three, surprised by a sudden and fierce fame. Crowds of men and women, in all the great cities of our land, hung upon his lips (during Moody and Sankey's first mission to Britain, 1873–75); innumerable lives opened their secrets to him, and made him aware of his power over them. When his first book (*Natural Law in the Spiritual World*) was published, he, being then about thirty-three, found another world at his feet: the great of the land thronged him, his social opportunities were boundless, and he was urged by the chief statesmen of our time to a political career. This is the kind of trial which one has seen wither some of the finest characters, and distract others from the simplicity and resolution of their youth. He passed through it unscathed. It neither warped his spirit nor turned him from his accepted vocation as a teacher of religion.

Again, in the end of his life, he was plunged to the opposite extreme. For two long years he not only suffered weakness and excruciating pain, but, what must have been more trying to a spirit like his, accustomed all his manhood to be giving, helping and leading, he became absolutely dependent on others. This also he bore unspoiled; and we who had known him from the beginning found him at the end the same humble, unselfish and cheerful friend, whom we loved when we sat together on the benches at college.

Perhaps the most conspicuous service which Henry Drummond rendered to his generation was to show them a Christianity which was perfectly natural. You met him somewhere, a graceful, well-dressed gentleman, tall and lithe, with a swing in his walk and a brightness on his face, who seemed to carry no cares and to know neither presumption nor timidity. You spoke, and found him keen for any of a hundred interests. He fished, he shot, he skated as few can, he played cricket; he would go any distance to see a fire or a football match. He had a new story, a new puzzle, or a new joke, every time he met you. Was it on the street? He drew you to watch two message-boys meet, grin, and knock each other's hats off, lay down their baskets, and enjoy a friendly chaffer of marbles. Was it on the train? He had dredged from the bookstall every paper and magazine that was new to him; or he would read you a fresh tale of his favourite, Bret Harte. Had you seen *Apostle of the*

Tules, or Frederic Harrison's article in the *Nineteenth Century* on 'Ruskin as a Master of English Prose', or Q's *Conspiracy aboard the Midas*, or the Badminton *Cricket* ? If it was a rainy afternoon in a country house, he described a new game, and in five minutes every body was in the thick of it. If it was a children's party, they clamoured for his sleight-of-hand. He smoked, he played billiards; lounging in the sun he could be the laziest man you ever saw.

If you were alone with him, he was sure to find out what interested you, and listen by the hour. The keen brown eyes got at your heart, and you felt you could speak your best to them. Sometimes you would remember that he was Drummond the evangelist, the author of books which measured their circulation by scores of thousands. Yet there was no assumption of superiority nor any ambition to gain influence – nothing but the interest of one healthy human being in another. If the talk slipped among deeper things, he was as untroubled and as unforced as before; there was never a glimpse of a phylactery nor a smudge of 'unction' about his religion. He was one of the purest, most unselfish, most reverent souls you ever knew; but you would not have called him saint. The name he went by among younger men was 'the Prince'; there was a distinction and a radiance upon him that compelled the title.

That he had 'a genius for friendship' goes without saying, for he was rich in the humility, the patience and the powers of trust, which such a genius implies. Yet his love had, too, the rarer and more strenuous temper which requires 'the common aspiration', is jealous for a friend's growth, and has the nerve to criticise. It is a measure of what he felt friendship to be that he has defined religion in terms of it. With such gifts, his friendship came to many men and women – women, to all of whom his chivalry and to some his gratitude and admiration were among the most beautiful aspects of his character. There was but one thing which any of his friends could have felt a want – others respected it as the height and crown of his friendship – and that was this.

The longer you knew him, the fact which most impressed you was that he seldom talked about himself, and, no matter how deep the talk might go, never about that inner self which for praise or for sympathy is in many men so clamant, and in all more or less perceptible. Through the radiance of his presence and the familiarity of his talk there sometimes stole out, upon those who were becoming his friends the sense of a great loneliness and silence behind, as when you catch a snow-peak across the summer fragrance and music of a Swiss meadow. For he always kept silence concerning his own religious struggles. He never asked even his most intimate friends for sympathy, nor seemed to carry any wound, however slight, that needed their fingers for his healing . . .

But we should greatly mistake the man and his teaching if we did not perceive that the source and return of all his interest in men and of all his trust in God was Jesus Christ. Of this his own words are most eloquent:

> The power to set the heart right, to renew the springs of action, comes from Christ. The sense of the infinite worth of the single soul, and the recoverableness of a man at his worst, are the gifts of Christ. The freedom from guilt, the forgiveness of sins, comes from Christ's cross; the hope of immortality springs from Christ's grave. Personal conversion means for life a personal religion, a personal trust in God, a personal dedication to his cause. These, brought about how you will, are supreme things to aim supreme losses if they are missed.

That was the conclusion of all his doctrine. There was no word of Christ more often upon his lips than this: 'Abide in Me and I in you, for without Me ye can do nothing.'

G. Adam Smith, *The Life of Henry Drummond* (1899), pp. 7–8.

Opinions differ greatly as to the worth of Henry Drummond's two best-sellers, *Natural Law in the Spiritual World* (1883) and *The Ascent of Man* (1894). They undoubtedly did something to lessen the estrangement of science and religion in the age of Darwin, Huxley and Tyndall, and attracted admiring comments from distinguished teachers like Professors Balfour Stewart, P. G. Tait and Archibald Geikie. But the long-term verdict is less enthusiastic, though as late as 1943 the eminent historian of science, Dr Joseph Needham, could say of *Natural Law* that it was 'a naïve work, but it has the naïvete of something fundamentally true'.

Today, Drummond (1851–97) is remembered not so much for his writings as for his uniquely fruitful work as an evangelist among students worldwide in the wake of the American missioners, Moody and Sankey – and for his almost magically attractive personality: the very embodiment, it seemed, of all the Christian graces. The tribute by Sir George Adam Smith, the distinguished Old Testament scholar who held office as Principal of Aberdeen University from 1909 until 1935, gives some idea of the impact made, particularly on young people, by Scottish Presbyterianism's Prince Charming.

Twentieth Century

❄ ❄ ❄
A SCOTTISH MISSIONARY IN WEST AFRICA c.1905

When I went to Calabar I heard a great deal about Miss Slessor, and naturally I wished to see her. She had been so courageous that I imagined she must be somewhat masculine, with a very commanding appearance, but I was pleasantly disappointed when I found she was a true woman, with a heart full of motherly affection Her welcome was the heartiest I received. Her originality, brightness, and almost girlish spirit fascinated me. One could not be long in her company without enjoying a right hearty laugh. As her semi-native house was just finished, and she always did with the minimum of furniture and culinary articles, the Council authorised me to take a filter, dishes, and cooking utensils from Akpap, and I had also provision cases and personal luggage. I was not sure what 'Ma' would say about sixteen loads arriving, because there were no wardrobes or presses, and one had just to live in one's boxes. When 'Ma' saw the filter she said, 'Ye maun a' hae yer filters noo-a-days. Filters werna created: they were an after-thocht.' She quite approved of my having it all the same.

Mail day was always a red-letter day. We only got letters fortnightly then. She was always interested in my home news, and told me hers, so that we generally had a very happy hour together. Then the papers would be read and their contents discussed. To be with her was an education. She had such a complete grasp of all that was going on in the world. One day after studying Efik for two hours she said to me, 'Lassie, you have had enough of that today, go away and read a novel for a short time.'

She was very childlike with her bairns and dearly loved them. One night I had to share her bed, and during the night felt her clapping me on the shoulder. I think she had been so used with black babies that this was the force of habit, for she was amused when I told her of it in the morning.

There was no routine with 'Ma'. One never knew what she would be doing. One hour she might be having a political discussion with a District Commissioner, the next supervising the building of a house, and later on judging native palavers. Late one evening I heard a good deal of talking and also the sound of working. I went in to see what was doing and there was 'Ma' making cement and the bairns spreading it on the floor with their hands in candlelight. The whole scene at so late an hour was too much for my gravity.

When at prayers with her children she would sometimes play a tambourine at the singing, and if the bairns were half asleep it struck their curly heads instead of her elbow.

Her outstanding characteristic was her great sympathy, which enabled her to get into touch with the highest and the lowest. Once while cycling together we met the Provincial Commissioner. After salutations and some conversation with him she finished up by saying, 'Good-bye, and see and be a guid laddie!'

While out walking one Sabbath we came across several booths where the natives who were making the Government road were living. She began chatting with them, and then told them the Parable of the Lost Sheep. She told everything in a graphic way, and with a perfect knowledge of the vernacular, and they followed her with reverence and intense interest all through. To most of them, if not to all, that would be the first time they had heard of a God of Love.

She had really two personalities. In the morning one would hear evil-doers getting hotly lectured for their 'fashions', and in the evening when all was quiet she lifted one up to the very heights regarding the things of the Kingdom. She always had a wonderful vision of what the power of the Gospel could make of the most degraded, though bound by the strongest chains of superstition and heathenism. One might enter her house feeling pessimistic, but one always left it an optimist.

W. P. Livingstone, *Mary Slessor of Calabar: Pioneer Missionary*
(1916), pp. 235–7.

This tribute by a visitor to Calabar may go some way to explaining the phenomenal influence which Mary Slessor (1848–1915) exerted in her corner of West Africa – as well as the reputation, second only to David Livingstone's, which she built up for herself in Church circles in Scotland in the last quarter of the nineteenth century and the first quarter of the twentieth. Sailing in 1876 for the Calabar coast of what is now Nigeria under the auspices of the United Presbyterian Church, this extraordinary woman gradually effected the transformation of an area noted for human sacrifice, twin murder and witchcraft, and won the loving respect of the inhabitants by her simple faith, her courage, her pioneering venturesomeness, and her sheer ability to survive in conditions which were as testing as the slums she had come from in Victorian Dundee. Unconventional, determinedly Scottish, and possessed of an indescribable strength and charm, she eventually won recognition as a magistrate from the British government; but her most notable achievement was no doubt the awed affection with which she was regarded by the people of her adopted country.

❦ ❦ ❦
ADVICE FROM A GREAT TRANSLATOR OF THE BIBLE

My last word to the reader is this. Do not rest content with curiously noting the differences between this version of the Bible and its predecessors, especially the Authorised English version, but try to understand and appreciate their common aim. The object of any translation ought to resemble the object of its original, and in this case it is not mere curiosity, not even intellectual interest. Our English Bibles always reprint the dedication of the 1611 version to King James; it is a somewhat fulsome piece of writing, nearly as fulsome as some of Bacon's references to that monarch. Why does nobody reprint the preface of 'the translators to the reader', which breathes an ampler air? Here are the concluding sentences of that neglected preface. 'It is a fearful thing to fall into the hands of the living God, but a blessed thing it is, and will bring us to everlasting blessedness in the end, when God speaketh unto us, to hearken; when he setteth his word before us, to read it; when he stretches out his hand and calleth to answer, Here am I, here we are to do thy will O God. The Lord work a care and conscience in us to know him, and serve him, that we may be acknowledged of him at the appearing of our Lord Jesus Christ, to whom with the Holy Ghost be all praise and thanksgiving', These words put nobly the chief end of reading the Bible, and the object of any version; it is to stir and sustain present faith in a living God who spoke and speaks. Three hundred years lie between the Authorised Version and the version printed in these pages, but I hope there is nothing in the execution, certainly there is nothing in the aim, of the modern translation which would be out of keeping with the tone of these searching words which preface its great predecessor.

J. Moffatt, Introduction to his Translation of the Bible (1926).

The twentieth century may not have too many outstanding religious achievements to its credit, in Scotland at any rate; but one which merits greater recognition than it generally receives is James Moffatt's astonishing, single-handed translation of the whole Bible, both Old and New Testaments. Moffatt (1870–1944) was not only a distinguished scholar who during his life-time held teaching posts on both sides of the Atlantic (at Mansfield College, Oxford, Trinity College, Glasgow and Union Theological Seminary, New York): he was also a deeply devoted Christian. In the 1926 introduction to his completed *magnum opus* he gives some characteristic advice.

❧ ❧ ❧

PROSPECTS THEN AND NOW

Fair and far the prospects I remember,
Far and fair;
Then 'twas June, but now alas! November
Chills the wintry air.

Then I hoped, but now is hope for stricken,
Then I feared, but now I know my doom;
Then I knew all impulses that quicken,
Now I see the tomb.

Fair and far the prospects I remember,
Fair and far;
Aye, but now I welcome dark December
As the Morning Star:

Then I hoped, but now on hope I reckon,
Then I feared, but now across the bar
Bright beyond the Darkness beckon
Prospects fair and far.

A. W. Mair, *Poems* (1934).

Faith, it need hardly be said, is not always an exuberant or exultant thing. One of its more muted moods is indicated in Robert Louis Stevenson's poem, 'If this were faith', where he asks the question,

> With the half of a broken hope for a pillow at night
> That somehow the right is the right
> And the smooth shall bloom from the rough:
> Lord, if that were enough?

The lines by Alexander William Mair (1875–1928), Professor of Greek in the University of Edinburgh from 1903 to 1928, are equally sober. But it can be argued that in their bleak hopefulness they come remarkably near to what Christian men and women in Scotland used to call 'the heart of the matter': the obstinate conviction that Good Friday was followed by Easter Day, and that 'he that loseth his life, the same shall find it'.

✺ ✺ ✺
ENCOUNTER WITH GOD

I cannot remember a time when my life seemed to me to be my own to do with as I pleased. From the very beginning its centre was not in itself or in me. I was of course, in the first instance, under the authority of the elder members of the household – so that in that as in other respects I was born a Presbyterian! I was under orders, and it was from my father or my mother or my nurse that the orders came. Yet my earliest memories clearly contain the knowledge that these elders did but transmit and administer an authority of which they were not themselves the ultimate source. For I never supposed that it was merely a case of my father's or mother's will being pitted against my will, still less of their power being pitted against my weakness. I knew that they had a *right* to ask of me what they did and that I had no right to refuse what they asked; that is, I knew that what they desired of me was right, and that my own contrary desire was wrong. But I knew also that their desiring it did not make it right, but that they desired it because it was already right independently of their desire. In other words, I understood that my parents were under the same constraint that they were so diligent in transferring to me. Not, of course, that this constraint dictated the selfsame actions and abstentions in them and in me. The little girl in *Punch*, who had justified her use of a certain unmaidenly expression by the plea that 'Daddy says it', only to be told that Daddy was Daddy, is reported to have replied, 'Well, I'm I'm.' My own father did not allow himself the use of such expressions, yet I understood very well that much was allowable for him that was not allowable for me, and that still more was incumbent on him that was not incumbent on me. But I knew also that in all this he was no more pleasing himself than he was allowing me to please myself. Had he given me the impression that it was merely his good pleasure I was called upon to obey, had he exercised an authority under which he showed no sign of standing himself, had he expected of me a way of life which bore no relation to his own way of living, his influence and authority over me could have had little of the character which in fact I felt them to possess. Actually, the way he himself lived, and the kind of being he was, exercised a more powerful and lasting constraint than all his spoken words of command.

I have been saying that I knew all this, and I think I did know it. This does not mean that I could then have explicitly formed in my mind any such propositions as the above, still less that I could have found words in which to express them. I could not then have isolated, with a view to contemplating them separately, any of the pieces of knowledge of which I have now spoken Yet I am quite sure that they were all implicitly present in my mind.

There came a day, indeed, when I was awakened to the limitations of my Presbyterian system by the discovery that elders are not infallible. In my case it was not by any means a rude awakening, but it was something of a shock none the less. There came a day and an occasion when it seemed clear to me that my mother was wrong in asking a certain thing of me and that I had some real justification for withholding obedience. Yet it is important to notice that this day could never have come if I had begun by supposing that my mother herself was the source of the authority which was given her to administer. Nor was the new situation which had emerged to be confused for a moment with a mere conflict of wills. That, unfortunately, would have been nothing new. What was new was the conflict of *judgements;* not that my parents wanted one thing of me while I wanted another thing for myself, but that my parents judged something to be *right* which I did not judge to be right for myself.

What then was the ultimate source of the authority which my parents were thus doing their fallible best to administer and under which they stood no less than I? What was this constraint that was laid on us? Whose was this greater will that we were both called upon to obey? Whom were my parents pleasing, since they were not pleasing themselves, and whom did they want me to please in pleasing them? Once again, I have no memory of a time when I did not know the answer. From the beginning I knew that it was God.

John Baillie, *Invitation to Pilgrimage* (1942), pp. 37–9.

MORNING PRAYER

O Thou who indwellest in our poor and shabby human life, lifting it now and then above the dominance of animal passion and greed, allowing it to shine with the borrowed lights of love and joy and peace, and making it a mirror of the beauties of a world unseen, grant that my part in the world's life today may not be to obscure the splendour of Thy presence but rather to make it more plainly visible to the eyes of my fellow men.

Let me stand today –
   for whatever is pure and true and just and good:
   for the advancement of science and education and true
      learning:
   for the redemption of daily business from the blight of self-
      seeking:
   for the rights of the weak and the oppressed:
   for industrial co-operation and mutual help:
   for the conservation of the rich traditions of the past:
   for the recognition of new workings of Thy Spirit in the minds of
      the men
   of my own time:
   for the hope of yet more glorious days to come.

Today, O Lord –
   let me put right before interest:
   let me put others before self:
   let me put the things of the spirit before the things of the body:
   let me put the attainment of noble ends above the enjoyment of
      present pleasures:
   let me put principle above reputation:
   let me put Thee before all else.

O Thou the reflection of whose transcendent glory did once appear unbroken in the face of Jesus Christ, give me today a heart like His – a brave heart, a true heart, a tender heart, a heart with great room in it, a heart fixed on Thyself; for His name's sake.

John Baillie, *A Diary of Private Prayer* (1936), p. 61.

※ ※ ※
EVENING PRAYER

O Thou who art the Lord of the night as of the day and to whose will all the stars are obedient, in this hour of darkness I too would submit my will to Thine.

> From the stirrings of self-will within my heart:
> From cowardly avoidance of necessary duty:
> From rebellious shrinking from necessary suffering:
> From discontentment with my lot:
> From jealousy of those whose lot is easier:
> From thinking lightly of the one talent Thou hast given me,
>   because Thou hast not given me five or ten:
> From uncreaturely pride:
> From undisciplined thought:
> From unwillingness to learn and un readiness to serve:
>   O God, set me free.

O God my Father, who art often closest to me when I am farthest from Thee, and who art near at hand when I feel that Thou hast forsaken me, mercifully grant that the defeat of my self-will may be the triumph in me of Thine eternal purpose.

> May I grow more sure of Thy reality and power:
> May I attain a clearer mind as to the meaning of my life on
>   earth:
> May I strengthen my hold upon life eternal:
> May I look more and more to things unseen:
> May my desires grow less unruly and my imaginations more
>   pure:
> May my love for my fellow men grow deeper and more tender,
>   and may I be
> more willing to take their burdens upon myself.

To thy care, O God, I commend my soul and the souls of all whom I love and who love me; through Jesus Christ our Lord. Amen.

John Baillie, A Diary of Private Prayer (1936), p. 131.

John Baillie (1886–1960) was almost certainly the outstanding Scottish theologian of the 1930s, 1940s and 1950s. After teaching for fifteen years in North America, he returned to his home country in 1934 as Professor of Divinity at New College in the University of Edinburgh. Between then and his retirement in 1956 he exerted a very wide influence as Moderator of the General Assembly (1943), convener of the Assembly's celebrated Commission for the Interpretation of God's Will in the Present Crisis (1942–6), one of the Presidents of the World Council of Churches (1952), Dean of the Faculty of Divinity and Principal of New College (1952–6), and participant in the negotiations which produced the 'Bishops Report' on Anglican–Presbyterian relations. He was made a Companion of Honour by the Queen in 1957.

True to the substance of historic Christianity if uneasy with some of its traditional formulations, he demonstrated his essential fidelity in the eloquent apologetic of *Invitation to Pilgrimage* (1942) and in *A Diary of Private Prayer* (1936), which rapidly became a devotional classic and has been often translated. Although he moved far from the unyielding Calvinism of his upbringing, he was always prepared (like his equally distinguished brother, Professor Donald Baillie of St Mary's College, St Andrews) to acknowledge his debt to the Free Church manse of Gairloch and to spell out the vital lessons which he believed it had taught him. These lessons are impressively touched upon in the accompanying extract from *Invitation to Pilgrimage*.

※ ※ ※
POSTSCRIPT TO AN AUTOBIOGRAPHY

Via, veritas, vita – the motto of the University of Glasgow. There, and elsewhere in the incomparable Fourth Gospel, is the absolute Wisdom in which alike to meet one's own perplexities, the mounting confusions of the world, despair and fear. Maybe mankind at last will find it; come at last through the symbolisms and hearsays of human intelligence to knowledge and worship of Him Who upholds all things by the word of His power; of whom all things consist; in Whom, as in the ether, we live and move and have our being . . .

Periodically, in writing these closing words, I have been conscious of speech and music from some nearby loudspeaker. But now, at this very moment, a song is in the air, and either the volume has been increased or hearing is by old association more acute.

To the haunting tune of Crimond the metrical version of the 23rd psalm is being spread over all the world from the Abbey of Westminster; from the wedding of the King's daughter:

> The Lord's my shepherd, I'll not want;
> He makes me down to lie
> In pastures green; he leadeth me
> The quiet waters by.

That age-old song of presbyterian Scotland, the national anthem of its faith. I see my mother trace its lines for me to read. I hear my father's voice: 'John, can you say the 23rd psalm yet?' I hear it sung at family worship in the manse; in the College Church in Glasgow; in the little highland conventicle of halcyon summer holidays. The Abbey of Westminster dissolves to the Kirk of Rothiemurchus.

Ite, missa est. In the porch one's eyes would straightway lift to the everlasting hills that stood round about; to the purple expansions of the heather moors; to the forests of larch and spruce and pine; to the snow-fed cataracts; to all the majesty and beauty of the highland scene where first there came the fateful stirrings to achieve. So homewards to the gentler landscape of the valley of the Spey. Here grassy knolls and silver birch; here whispering corn edged bright with yellow marigolds; here softer flow of tributary stream. Green pastures and quiet waters. Out of the wind.

J. C. W. Reith, *Into the Wind* (1949), pp. 530–1.

John Charles Walsham Reith, 1st Baron Reith of Stonehaven (1889–1971), served an engineering apprenticeship in Glasgow and entered the field of radio communication. He became first general manager of the British Broadcasting Corporation in 1922 and its director-general from 1927 to 1938. His later years were somewhat anti-climactic, though he was MP for Southampton (1940), Minister of Works and Buildings (1940–42) and Chairman of the Commonwealth Communications Board (1946–50).

An immensely able autocrat who stamped his personality on pre-war broadcasting, he never felt adequately recognised or (to use his own word) 'stretched', and there is a wistful melancholy about his autobiographical writings. This passage from the conclusion of *Into the Wind* speaks not only of the great man's regrets but also of the faith which, as a son of the manse, he still felt able to express in the words of that much-loved focus of Scottish piety, the 23rd Psalm.

❧ ❧ ❧
PORTRAIT OF A BORDER MINISTER,
BY HIS SON

My father, as you may remember, was a large, tranquil man. (I have known an eager Edinburgh reporter describe him as 'huge'.) He was usually grave, but cheerful, with a tremendous laugh in him on occasions, when he threw himself from side to side in sheer abandonment. In this he was like his brother John, of whom it has been said that he once laughed so heartily that the chair on which he was sitting subsided, and he was 'seen still sitting jubilant amid the ruins'. My father enjoyed humour in others and saw the humorous side of people, but did not jest himself. He was slow in expressing affection for any of us, but we were all perfectly aware of his deep and abiding love for us, and once, I can remember, when I was ill and suffering as a child, an expression of it that I never forgot. Punishments in our house were *very* rare, and yet there was a certain awe in our affection for him. I never knew anyone who took liberties with him, and as he grew older he became a very venerable figure, whom the whole region recognised as a kind of 'Father in God' . . . He knew how to handle human beings. He never once in his long ministry of forty-five years in Stitchel had even a vote in his Session, and he never spoke in the United Presbyterian Synod save once, as an old man, and then I think it was in favour of giving extended influence in church affairs to women. An on political matters, as I look back, he seems, to me at least, to have been *almost* invariably right!

All his life he was content with a small country church, which was liker one large family than any congregation I have ever known. Population diminished greatly in the district during that period, and I think he had in consequence to face the long ordeal of seeing it diminish to little more than half of its original membership. But he never, I believe, sought any change. He had no ambition except to do the work for which God had, as he believed, chosen and trained him and to which, as all his church then believed, he had been called also by God through the voice of the people. Since this was so, he felt he was called to remain where he was, and unless an equally clear Voice called him away, he did not feel at liberty to move.

When I read Carlyle's fine description of the Seceder ministers of his youth, I am always reminded of my father . . .

His main interests were in his church and his people and his family and he always took the large and patient view. He was a true father to every one of us. When he died, though I was in full middle life, I felt like a little child again, lost and out in the rain.

When I saw him lying dead, I was amazed at the quiet grandeur of his face. He looked like one of the great ones of the earth. It was a reminder that real greatness is not a thing of outward circumstance and that it is possible to live greatly in what the world would think a very limited sphere of labour. I remember, too, as I looked at him, it suddenly flashed upon me what a living message from God Himself he had been to me all my days, of far more real meaning to a free human spirit than any articulate thunder could have been, even though it spoke my name. After all, a human being is a far richer means of Divine expression than any natural force or thing could possibly be. Here from my earliest childhood had been one beside me influencing me in a thousand gentle ways in favour of uprightness, kindness, unselfishness and faith, making it easier at every stage for me to believe in goodness and in God. God Himself had all my life through my father telling me how He felt towards me and how he would have me think and act.

I never pass his birthplace in the little forester's cottage in the Penmanshiel wood without a glow of thankfulness in my heart and a reassurance about this Power behind the Universe and its meaning and its end. I look out for it always as I draw near it in the train and salute it as I pass!

David Cairns, *An Autobiography* (1950), pp. 45–8.

The history of modern Scottish piety would be a much poorer thing were it not for the massive contribution of four or five great families: the Erskines, the Browns, the MacLeods, the Cairnses and the Baillies. Interestingly enough, the Cairnses and the Browns intermarried, and the outstanding representative in modern times of their peculiar genius was David Smith Cairns (1862–1946), minister of the United Presbyterian Church at Ayton from 1895, and professor of Dogmatics and Apologetics in the United Free Church College (later Christ's College) at Aberdeen from1907 to 1937. There is a kind of magic about his prose, nowhere more discernible than in his heart-felt tribute to his father, minister for 45 years of the little Borders congregation at Stitchel.

❦ ❦ ❦
CHRISTIAN WITHOUT KNOWING IT

During those years [the late 1930s] I wrote very little poetry . . . Meanwhile the world was darkening, and our work was growing precarious. Then my wife fell ill and had to go into a nursing home. After she began to recover, I was returning from the nursing home one day – it was the last day of February 1939 – when I saw some schoolboys playing at marbles on the pavement; the old game had 'come round again' at its own time known only to children, and it seemed a simple little rehearsal for a resurrection, promising a timeless renewal of life. I wrote in my diary next day:

Last night, going to bed alone, I suddenly found myself (I was taking off my waistcoat) reciting the Lord's Prayer in a loud emphatic voice – a thing I had not done for many years – with deep urgency and profound disturbed emotion. While I went on I grew more composed; as if it had been empty and craving and were being replenished, my soul grew still; every word had a strange fullness of meaning which astonished and delighted me. It was late; I had sat up reading; I was sleepy; but as I stood in the middle of the floor half-undressed, saying the prayer over and over, meaning after meaning sprang from it, overcoming me again with joyful surprise; and I realised that this simple petition was always universal and always inexhaustible, and day by day sanctified life.

I had believed for many years in God and the immortality of the soul; I had clung to the belief even when, in horrifying glimpses, I saw animals peeping through human eyes. My belief receded then, it is true, to an unimaginable distance, but it still stood there, not in any territory of mine, it seemed, but in a place of its own. Now I realised that, quite without knowing it, I was a Christian, no matter how bad a one; and I remembered a few days later that Janet Adam Smith had told me, half-teasingly, while I was staying in Hampstead, that my poetry was Christian poetry; the idea had then been quite strange to me. I had a vague sense during these days that Christ was the tuning-point of time and the meaning of life to everyone, no matter what his conscious beliefs; to my agnostic friends as well as Christians. I read the New Testament many times during the following months, particularly the Gospels. I did not turn to any church, and my talks with ministers and divines cast me back upon the Gospels again, which was probably the best thing that could have happened I had no conception of the splendours of

Christendom; I remained quite unaware of them until some years later I
was sent by the British Council to Italy.

E. Muir, *An Autobiography* (1954), pp. 245–7.

Twentieth-century Scotland's drift away from its traditional faith is illustrated by the fact that of the four greatest literary figures then living
only one could by any stretch of the imagination be called a Christian.
James Leslie Mitchell (Lewis Grassic Gibbon), whom one recent biographer
described as 'Blasphemer and Reformer', was a scientific rationalist and an
atheist. Hugh Macdiarmid was part-Marxist, part-Nationalist, though always
a bit of a chameleon. Neil Gunn in his later years dabbled in Zen Buddhism.
Only Edwin Muir (1887–1959) provides an exception to what seems to be
the rule – and even in his case it is to Catholic rather than Protestant Christianity to which, after years in the wilderness, he returns.

❦ ❦ ❦
A LIFE SURVEYED

What is left to say when one has come to the end of writing about one's life? Some kind of development, I suppose, should be expected to emerge, but I am very doubtful of such things, for I cannot bring life into a neat pattern. If there is a development in my life – and that seems an idle supposition – then it has been brought about more by things outside than by any conscious intention of my own. I was lucky to spend my first fourteen years in Orkney; I was unlucky to live afterwards in Glasgow as a Displaced Person; until at last I acquired a liking for that plain, warm-hearted city. Because a perambulating revivalist preacher came to Kirkwall when I was a boy, I underwent an equivocal religious conversion there; because I read Blatchford in Glasgow, I repeated the experience in another form, and found myself a Socialist. In my late twenties I came, by chance, under the influence of Nietzsche. In my early thirties I had the good fortune to meet my wife, and have had since the greater good fortune of sharing my life with her. In my middle thirties I became aware of immortality, and realised that it gave me a truer knowledge of myself and my neighbours. Years later in St. Andrews I discovered that I had been a Christian without knowing it. In Czechoslovakia I saw a whole people lost by one of the cruel turns of history, and exiled from themselves in the heart of their own country. I discovered in Italy that Christ had walked the earth, and also that things truly made preserve themselves through time in the first freshness of their nature. Now and then during these years I fell into the dumps for short or long periods, was subject to fears which I did not understand, and passed through stretches of blankness and deprivation. From these I learned things which I could not otherwise have learned, so that I cannot regard them as mere loss. Yet I believe that I would have been better without them.

When we talk of our development I fancy we mean little more than that we have changed with the changing world; and if we are writers or intellectuals, that our ideas have changed with the changing fashions of thought, and therefore not always for the better. I think that if any of us examines his life, he will find that most good comes to him from a few loyalties, and a few discoveries made many generations before he was born, which always must be made anew. These too must sometimes appear to come by chance, but in the infinite web of things and events chance must be different from what we think it to be. To comprehend that is not given to us, and to think of it is to recognise a mystery, and to acknowledge the necessity of faith. As I look back on the part of the mystery which is my own life, my own fable, what I am most aware of is that we receive more than we can ever give; we receive it from the past, on which we draw with every breath, but also – and this is a point of faith from the Source of the mystery itself, by the means which religious people call grace.

E. Muir, *An Autobiography* (1954), pp. 280–1.

Edwin Muir writes so attractively that a second passage from his autobiography compels inclusion. It indicates very clearly that the return to the Lord's Prayer was no passing or isolated incident.

✼ ✼ ✼
TWO CELEBRATIONS OF COMMUNION

The circumstances which initiated my reconsideration of the central fact of the Christian Gospel, the love of God, were twofold, and they were both associated with the Sacrament of Holy Communion. The first celebration took place in a lonely parish Church in the Highlands of Scotland. Some seventy people had gathered for what has always been the most solemn religious action of the Church of Jesus Christ, in any part of the world but more intensely in these parts. The sermon preached by a visiting minister unfolded the whole glory of God's love to men and women, in that while we were yet sinners Christ died for us. He concluded his sermon with the Gospel invitation to all who truly repent to receive of the grace of God. Thereafter, the Kirk Session entered in procession, bearing the bread and wine of the Sacrament, by Our Lord's own institution the outward and visible signs of His real presence with us. The first act of the next part of the service was not, however, an invitation to all who truly repent to close with the Gospel offer of the sermon. On the contrary, there took place a lengthy recital of several lists of heinous sins, drawn from the Scriptures undoubtedly, with a terrifying warning that if anyone were guilty of any of these sins, he could eat the bread and drink the cup to his eternal damnation. Because this process of 'fencing the tables' had been taking place for generations, and had created a deep fear of the consequences of possible hypocrisy, only four of the seventy in the congregation dared to come forward into the pews spread with white linen for this occasion. The service which has mediated the love of God to Christian believers for centuries was stultified at the very point where it should have had its greatest power and meaning. It was as if for these worshippers the holiness of God had become a screen to obscure His infinite love; or, more seriously still, as if His love were so holy that it could not abide the presence of sinners.

The second circumstance which compelled me to reconsider how we ought as Christians to think about the love of God was a celebration of this same Sacrament, a hemisphere away from the first, in a hospital in Sydney, Australia. There were four of us present: the patient, George, with his mother, a student-minister and myself. As I conducted the service, the student-minister wrote the words I spoke on George's bare shoulder. Seven years before, George, who had been till then a normally active young man, became paralysed, becoming blind and deaf. He had to lie completely flat on his back. Gradually, they discovered that it was possible to have communication with George through writing words upon his shoulder. George was about seventeen when it all happened. In the depth of this silence and suffering, George decided that he wished to join the full membership of the Church, and to receive catechetical training. This he had received; he had been confirmed and the time had come for his first Communion. We four shared it together in a side-ward of the hospital. Never have I been so profoundly conscious of the encompassing cloud of witnesses or of the near Presence. As we proceeded slowly, sentence by sentence, word by word, we had ample opportunity to ponder every word of the Sacramental service. Under God's mercy one man's faith had taken us closer to the heart of God's love than any demonstration by thousands whose faith had come to them in easier conditions.

It was the juxtaposition of those two celebrations which generated the subject of the present discussion. On the one hand, the situation which had been designed by Our Lord as the supreme means of grace and the bodying forth of His love had become confused in intention. Those who had long ago been invited to 'taste and see that the Lord is good' had been prevented at the moment when the cup was on the point of being raised to their lips. Certainly the inner logic of the service demanded that the Gospel call to grace should be sealed in the receiving of the Sacrament. The fact that in the fourth century the ancient Church may have 'fenced the tables' according to the Clementine Liturgy in no way mitigates the problem. On the other hand, one of the many things which must strike us in George's story is the fact that the suffering and sorrow which are traditionally offered as arguments against the existence of a loving God constituted the circumstances in which George found, and was found by, God. Where men have said in every generation God cannot be, there for George God was. What, then, is the love of God, which can be concealed in the place where God through Christ willed it to be most unmistakeably discerned, and which for one man at least, standing in the tradition of the Epistle to the Hebrews chapters eleven and twelve, can be manifest in the cloud and thick darkness of the soul's distress? Is there any single conception of the love of God which will enable us fully to describe what has happened in these two events in which for me this essay was generated? In a word, how are we to think about and describe the love of God?

John McIntyre, *On the Love of God* (1962), pp. 9–11 .

In the Scottish reformers' *Book of Common Order* (1564), 'The Manner of Administration of the Lord's Supper' has near its beginning the famous exhortation which has become known as 'The fencing of the tables'. After recalling how St Paul 'exhorted all persons diligently to try and examine themselves before they presume to eat of that bread, and to drink of that cup', the minister excludes from communion all wrong-doers, 'such as live a life fighting against the will of God' – but then continues: 'And yet this I pronounce not, to seclude any penitent person, how grievous soever his sins before have been, so, that he feel in his heart unfeigned repentance for the same; but only such as continue in sin without repentance' (see p. 15). In later times, and particularly in the West Highlands of Scotland, the cataloguing of sins tended to stifle the welcome accorded to penitent sinners, with the result that in many congregations only a small minority dared to communicate. It is this – still continuing – practice to which John McIntyre refers in this extract from his study, *On the Love of God*.

After parish ministry in the West of Scotland, and some years as a professor in Australia, John McIntyre (1916–2005) succeeded John Baillie in the Chair of Divinity at New College, the University of Edinburgh, in 1956. He soon won renown not only as an eminent theologian with a succession of learned publications to his credit, but as a superbly able administrator who became Dean of Divinity and Principal of New College, and twice served as acting Principal of the University. The motivation for all his service is disclosed in this passage from one of his earlier works.

※ ※ ※

TO THE GOD WHO IS EVERYWHERE

From Psalm 139

Thou art before me, Lord, thou art behind,
And thou above me hast spread out thy hand;
Such knowledge is too wonderful for me,
Too high to grasp, too great to understand.

Then whither from thy Spirit shall I go,
And whither from thy presence shall I flee?
If I ascend to heaven thou art there,
And in the lowest depths I meet with thee.

If I should take my flight into the dawn,
If I should dwell on ocean's farthest shore,
Thy mighty hand would rest upon me still,
And thy right hand would guard me evermore.

If I should say, 'Darkness will cover me,
And I shall hide within the veil of night',
Surely the darkness is not dark to thee,
The night is as the day, the darkness light.

Search me, O God, search me and know my heart,
Try me, O God, my mind and spirit try;
Keep me from any path that gives thee pain,
And lead me in the everlasting way.

Ian Pitt-Watson in *The Church Hymnary* (3rd edn, 1973), no. 68.

O ne of the outstanding ministers of his generation, Ian Robertson Pitt-Watson served in succession as Chaplain to Aberdeen University, minister of St James's, Forfar and of New Kilpatrick (Bearsden), and Professor of Practical Theology in Aberdeen before moving to Fuller Theological Seminary in the USA, where he died in 1995. He was not only an able scholar, distinguished in philosophy and theology, and an impressive preacher, lecturer and writer, but a fine musician who even in his undergraduate days made his name as conductor of a well-known group of student singers. His translation into modern English (based on the *New English Bible*) of one of the greatest of the Psalms has already established itself in contemporary worship. Published in the third edition of the *Church Hymnary* in 1973, it witnesses to the continuing power of a meditation from ancient Israel on the omnipresence of God.

❦ ❦ ❦
FOR ONE WHO HAS REALISED
THAT HE IS GROWING OLD

O God,
It seems like yesterday
that I went out to work for the first time;
and now I haven't much longer to go,
and I'm well over the half-way line.
I can't shut my eyes to the fact
that I'm getting older.
Physically, I get more easily tired,
and any effort becomes more and more of an effort.
Mentally, I'm slower;
I can't work for so long a time;
and concentration is more difficult.
First and foremost, help me to realise quite clearly
what I can do and what I can't do,
and to accept my necessary limitations.
And then help me to be thankful
for all that the years have given me,
and for all the experience that
life has brought me.
Help me to use what is left to me of life
wisely and well;
for time is short now
and I dare not waste any of it.

Let me remember what the prophet said:
Your old men shall dream dreams
And your young men shall see visions. *Joel 2.28*

Long as my life shall last,
Teach me thy way!
Where'er my lot be cast,
Teach me thy way!
Until the race is run,
Until the journey's done,
Until the crown is won,
Teach me thy way!

William Barclay, *Prayers for Help and Healing* (1968), p. 54.

William Barclay (1907–78), the author of this prayer, was probably the best-known of all Protestant clergymen in Scotland during the second half of the twentieth century – celebrated not only for his numerous publications, including the volumes of his *Daily Study Bible* (which won widespread acclaim as masterpieces of scholarly popularisation), but for his inimitable performances on radio and television. Though born in Wick, he spent most of his life in the Glasgow area, first as minister of Trinity Church of Scotland in Renfrew, and then as lecturer and ultimately Professor of Divinity and Biblical Criticism in Trinity College, the University of Glasgow's Faculty of Divinity. A superb teacher, he had a typically West-of-Scotland manner and attitude, unpretentious and approachable, and his learning was always lightly worn and skilfully deployed in the service of a liberal and persuasive interpretation of the Christian faith.

His prayer about growing old is typical of the down-to-earth practicality and spiritual insight which marked all his work and accounted for the affection and admiration with which he was almost universally regarded.

✻ ✻ ✻
AN ORCADIAN'S FAITH

I think everyone, if he or she thinks about it at all, is aware of two wills at work. The personal will seeks security and power and love and success. There are strong minds with distinct aims in view that can carry a person a fair distance along the road of heart's desire; but there are always accidents and imponderables that turn the stern face another way. Before 1789, would not Napoleon Bonaparte have been content with a captain's insignia? In an Elizabethan playhouse, what happened when a manager said to the country boy from Stratford, 'Here, Will, you have a way with words. See if you can patch up this old play somewhat'?

There is I think another will that we have no control over. A shaping divinity takes over from our rough-hewings. It 'prevents us everywhere', as Eliot says, but it also offers opportunities beyond anything we could have hoped for. We are hardly aware of the daily operatings, but looking back over one's life there are, it seems to me, clear evidences of the shaping spirit, whose 'preventing' we might have resented at the time; and, whenever it opened good new prospects for us, we attributed them to luck, or, more dangerously, to strengths and subtleties in ourselves that we were not aware of; we think then of ourselves as masters of our fate.

Great power corrupts absolutely, in part because the man of destiny thinks at last that the source of power rises from his inherent merits. But one of the most powerful men of modern times, Napoleon, could admit that the Paternoster is a transcendent sublimity: 'Thy Kingdom come. Thy will be done. Give us this day our daily bread . . .'.

To lose one's own will in the will of God should be the true occupation of every man's time on earth. Only a few of us – the saints – are capable of that simplicity.

We are all one, saint and sinner. Everything we do sets the whole web of creation trembling, with light or with darkness. It is an awesome thought, that a good word spoken might help a beggar in Calcutta or a burning child in Burundi; or conversely. But there is beauty and simplicity in it, sufficient to touch our finite minds.

I say, once a day at least, 'Saint Magnus, pray for us . . .'.

George Mackay Brown, *For the Islands I Sing* (1994), pp. 185–7.

Born at Stromness in 1921 and dying there in 1996, George Mackay Brown never left Orkney for long, though he studied English at Newbattle Abbey College (under Edwin Muir) and Edinburgh University. A prey to alcoholism in earlier years, he came to live a life of great productivity, pouring out novels, short stories, poems and essays, all of which – to quote a modern commentator – 'move towards ideal and undoubtedly metaphysical conclusions'. They are also marked by a rare simplicity and charm. His conversion to Catholicism can be seen as central to his intellectual and spiritual development.

❆ ❆ ❆
PRAYER FROM IONA

Be thou, triune God, in the midst of us as we give thanks for those who have gone from the sight of earthly eyes. They, in Thy nearer presence, still worship with us in the mystery of the one family in heaven and on earth.

We remember those whom Thou didst call to high office, as the world counts high. They bore the agony of great decisions and laboured to fashion the Ark of the Covenant nearer to Thy design.

We remember those who, little recognised in the sight of men, bore the heat and burden of the unrecorded day. They served serene because they knew Thou hadst made them priests and kings, and now shine as the stars forever.

If it be Thy holy will, tell them how we love them, and how we miss them, and how we long for the day when we shall meet with them again.

God of all comfort, we lift into Thine immediate care those recently bereaved, who sometimes in the night time cry, 'Would God it were morning' and in the morning cry 'would God it were night'

Lift from their eyes the too distant vision of the resurrection at the last day. Alert them to hear the voice of Jesus saying, 'I AM Resurrection and I AM life': that they may believe this.

Strengthen them to go on in loving service to all Thy children. Thus shall they have communion with Thee and, in Thee, with their beloved. Thus shall they come to know, in themselves, that there is no death and that only a veil divides, thin as gossamer.

G. F. MacLeod, *The Whole Earth Shall Cry Glory: Iona Prayers* (1985), p. 60.

No one exercised a greater influence – whether by attraction or repulsion – on the religious life of twentieth-century Scotland than George Fielden MacLeod (1895–1991). Born into an upper-class Glasgow family, with many distinguished clerical ancestors, he was educated at Winchester and the Universities of Oxford and Edinburgh, served in the First World War (MC and Croix de Guerre), and became minister in succession of the prestigious city charges of St Cuthbert's, Edinburgh and (on the eve of the Great Depression) Govan Old, Glasgow, where his preaching attracted large congregations. In 1938, inspired by views later given expression to in his *We Shall Rebuild* and *Only One Way Left*, he founded the Iona Community to rebuild the living quarters of the ancient abbey on the island and to prepare young ministers for service in the most difficult parishes of industrial Scotland. From then onwards he was hardly ever out of the public eye, and the Community eventually grew into an ecumenical fellowship with a wide range of activities and interests, not only in Scotland but much further afield.

In his later years MacLeod was loaded with honours, both civil and ecclesiastical. He became Moderator of the General Assembly in 1957, and ten years thereafter he was elevated to the House of Lords as Lord MacLeod of Fuinary.

This prayer from *The Whole Earth Shall Cry Glory: Iona Prayers* reveals the celebrated preacher, who was also a combative pacifist, controversial advocate of Socialism and tireless campaigner against the 'nuclear deterrent', as an imaginative and eloquent leader of worship whose Celtic affinities are clearly discernible.

Acknowledgements

p.2 On the Resurrection of Christ;
reproduced from *Poems of William Dunbar*, ed. W. Mackay Mackenzie (1932) by permission of Faber and Faber Ltd.

p.4 A Spiritual Love-Song;
reproduced from *The Gude and Godlie Ballatis*, ed. I. Ross (1940/ 1957) by permission of The Saltire Society, Edinburgh.

p.6 Faith (Not 'Works') the Essential;
p.10 A Martyr's Last Words;
p.12 A Protestant Manifesto;
reproduced from *John Knox's History of the Reformation in Scotland, vol. 2*, ed. By W. C. Dickinson (1949) and published by Thomas Nelson. We have been unable to trace the rights holder.

p.30 The National Covenant;
reproduced from *Source Book of Scottish History, vol.3* ed. By W.C. Dickinson and G. Donaldson (1954) and published by Thomas Nelson. We have been uable to trace the rights holder.

p.69 The Joys of Heaven;
reproduced from *The World to Come and Final Destiny*, J. H. Leckie (1918) by kind permission of Continuum International Publishing Group.

p.76 Sir Walter Scott's Philosophy;
reproduced from *Sir Walter Scott*, John Buchan (1932) by permission of A P Watt Ltd on behalf of The Lord Tweedsmuir and Jean, Lady Tweedsmuir.

p.108 A Victorian Hero: Henry Drummond;
reproduced from *The Life of Henry Drummond* by G. Adam Smith (1899) by kind permission of Professor Andrew Roberts.

p.114 Advice from a Great Translator of the Bible;
despite our efforts we have been unable to race the current rights holder
for this extract from the Introduction to James Moffatt's *Translation of
the Bible* (1926, London). It is available in an edition reprinted by Kregel
Publications, PO Box 2607, Grand Rapids, Michigan 49501-2607, USA.

p.118 Encounter with God;
reproduced from *Invitation to Pilgrimage* by John Baillie (1942) by kind
permission of Oxford University Press.

pp.120–1 Morning Prayer & Evening Prayer;
reproduced from *A Diary of Private Prayer* by John Baillie (1936) by kind
permission of Oxford University Press.

p.123 Postscript to an Autobiography;
reproduced from *Into the Air* by JCW Reith (Copyright © Estate of JCW
Reith 1949) by permission of PFD (www.pfd.co.uk) on behalf of the Estate
of JCW Reith.

p.125 Portrait of a Border Minister by his Son;
reproduced from *David Cairns: An Autobiography, some recollections of a
long life and selected letters* edited by his son and daughter (1950) by kind
permission of SCM Press.

p.128 Christian Without Knowing It;
p.130 A Life Surveyed;
reproduced from *An Autobiography* by Edwin Muir (1954) published
by The Hogarth Press. Reprinted by permission of The Random House
Group.

p.132 Two Celebrations of Communion;
despite our efforts we have been unable to trace the rights holder of this
material from *On the Love of God* by John McIntyre published by Collins
(1962).

p.135 To the God who is Everywhere;
reproduced by kind permission of the Executors of the late Revd Ian Pitt-
Watson.

p.136 For One who has Realised that he is Growing Old;
reproduced from *Prayers for Help and Healing* by William Barclay (© 1968)
by kind permission of HarperCollins Publishers Ltd.

p.138 An Orcadian's Faith;
reproduced from *For the Islands I Sing* by George Mackay Brown (1994)
by permission of John Murray (Publishers).

p.140 Prayer from Iona;
'A Veil Thin as Gossamer' from *The Whole Earth Shall Cry Glory: Iona
Prayers* © 1985 published by Wild Goose Publications, Glasgow G2 3DH,
Scotland. Reproduced by permission.